LIVING WITH
CANNIBALS
AND OTHER WOMEN'S
ADVENTURES

SLUNG, MICHELE B., 1947 -

Illustrations by Elizabeth Traynor

Map Illustration by Dennis O'Brien

Library of Congress Cataloging-in-Publication Data

Slung, Michele B., 1947-
      Living with cannibals and other women's adventures / Michele Slung ;
foreword by Reeve Lindbergh.
        p. cm.
      ISBN 0-7922-7686-8
      1. Women explorers. 2. Voyages and travels. I. Title.
      G200 .S68 2000   99-087458

FOLLOWING PAGES: *Biruté Galdikas, immersed for the past
three decades in a field study of the orangutan inhabitants of Borneo's
Tanjung Puting Reserve, paddles through a pine thicket in 1973. She is
accompanied by Sugito, the first in a long line of orangutans in the
process of being returned to the wild.*

ROD BRINDAMOUR

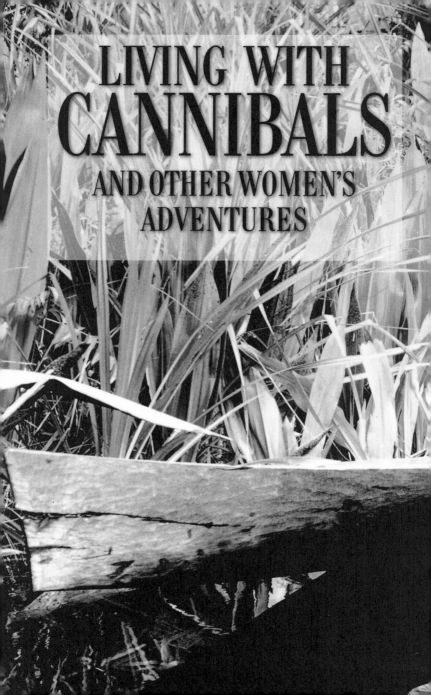

LIVING WITH
CANNIBALS
AND OTHER WOMEN'S
ADVENTURES

MICHELE SLUNG
FOREWORD BY REEVE LINDBERGH

ADVENTURE PRESS
NATIONAL GEOGRAPHIC SOCIETY
WASHINGTON, D.C.

For Cindy Derway,
explorer of heart and spirit

Nor Mountain hinder Me
Nor Sea —
Who's Baltic —
Who's Cordillera?

EMILY DICKINSON

CONTENTS

LIVING WITH
CANNIBALS
AND OTHER WOMEN'S
ADVENTURES

INTRODUCTION

Reeve Lindbergh

"Travelers are always discoverers," wrote my mother, Anne Morrow Lindbergh, in the first chapter of *North to the Orient*, her 1935 book describing the exploratory flight she and my father made together as pioneer aviators, over the "Great Circle Route," the polar route to Asia. "Our route was new; the air untraveled; the conditions unknown; the stories mythical."

This was the beginning of my mother's global exploration, and the beginning, too, of her inward exploration, the deeply thoughtful work that inspired her writing for a lifetime. I think that her survey flights over the Earth's surface in the 1930s paralleled an inward survey of her own growing confidence and capability, not only in writing, but also in aviation, a field only a few women had entered during that era. A quiet, studious diplomat's daughter, she became a flyer and an explorer, a radio operator and a navigator, and in 1930 among the first women to obtain a glider pilot's license in America. Through all of these adventures, she wrote down her impressions and experiences, and has left for us an eloquent record of the day-to-day life of a writer who was also a pilot: a woman who loved words and wings.

For my mother, as for the women explorers represented in this extraordinary collection, the outer and the inner explorer were connected, even reflective of one another. The farther she traveled, explored, and understood the Earth beneath her wings, the more competent she became as a pilot, and as a writer. Every woman in this book, I suspect, has traveled that same dual path of

By 1934, Anne Morrow Lindbergh had accompanied her husband,
Charles A. Lindbergh, on flights covering more than 40,000 miles

discovery, each in her own way. This is equally true for a
19th-century British globe-trotter and travel writer like
Isabella Bird Bishop and a contemporary world traveler
like Ireland's Dervla Murphy, who bicycled across Europe
to India in the 1960s, offering as a rationale simply, "If
someone enjoys cycling and wishes to go to India, the
obvious thing is to cycle there."

The single most important discovery for women
explorers may be the freedom that lies at the heart of
the very act of exploration. I learned from my mother that
for a woman of her day, this was unlike any other experience. She also cautioned us, in her writing and in her

across five continents. Recognizing her courageous spirit, the National Geographic Society that year awarded her its Hubbard Gold Medal.

reminiscences, that such "freedom" could be purchased only by meticulous planning and discipline. "The contingencies to be provided for were many and varied," she wrote. "We must consider the possibility of a parachute jump, and carry in our flying-suit pockets the most concentrated food and the most compact first-aid kit. We must be prepared for a forced landing in the North, where we would need warm bedding and clothes, and in the South, where we ought to have an insect-proof tent; and on the ocean, where we would need, in addition to food, plenty of fresh water."

Still, for the early women aviators—for my mother, for Amelia Earhart, for Beryl Markham, for Harriet Quimby, and especially for Bessie Coleman, first licensed African American aviator in the world—there must have been a radical kind of revelation in their first flights, a wonderfully subversive understanding that here, at least, there could be no considerations of gender or race, no social concepts of "woman's place." In the air there was no such thing as society, at all. Nothing mattered except the airplane, the skill of the person who flew it, and the limitless sky.

Even before airplanes were invented, the explorer's freedom must have been especially appealing to 19th-century women whose domestic lives were proscribed and confined to a degree almost unimaginable today. They could not vote in some countries, were not encouraged to seek higher education, rarely held public office, and were severely limited in the right to own property and to retain custody and control of their children. Compared to these restrictions, the risks of travel must have seemed paltry to the feminine imagination.

For a number of women adventurers, born to wealth or blessed with an early inheritance, there was the added freedom of comfortable financial circumstances. In Victorian times, especially, privilege was often a prerequisite for adventure, although the adventures themselves might include hardships and dangers unknown to those members of the privileged class who stayed safely at home.

But, whether privileged or not, by anyone's standards the women here described are not creatures of comfort or complacency. Some have vehemently proclaimed their causes, aims, and political agendas as they traversed bleak wastelands or scaled daunting heights, like turn-of-the-century traveler Fanny Bullock Workman, who held up a sign advocating "Votes For Women!" as she stood 2,000 feet above sea level on a remote Asian glacier. Others live their convictions now, in our own time, every day. Dr. Sylvia A. Earle, a modern oceanographer of world-wide reputation, makes no secret of the fact that she dedicates herself and her work to "the fishes," and to the health and preservation of her beloved oceans.

Other women explorers have felt propelled by equally strong, yet more intangible forces. For these women, exploration and travel and work may represent, in the words of Biruté Galdikas, "not just a scientific but a spiritual quest." There is a subtle impulse to understand the here and now, to become familiar with the ephemeral nature of life as it exists at a certain point in history, "to capture some of the magic," as my mother rather wistfully put it, of the moment when explorers open the world in a whole new way, and in doing so change it irrevocably, as all explorers inevitably do.

The early aviators arguably changed the world to a greater extent than any other explorers have ever done. "A few years earlier, from the point of view of aircraft alone, it would have been impossible to reach these places; a few years later, and there will be no such isola-tion," my mother wrote about the territory and the people she and my father encountered on their exploratory flights in the 1930s. Thirty years later, both she and my father took stock of the changes brought about by air travel and advancing technology, and became concerned.

In the 1960s they traveled the globe together again, this time in an effort to protect the Earth's wild places and wild creatures now threatened by the very accessibility she and her aviator husband had helped to create. Much of my mother's later writing focused upon the irreplaceable value of life in all its forms, as in an essay she wrote about a trip to Africa with my father, published as part of a book called *Earthshine.* "Wilderness is threatened everywhere. The extinction of animals is not the only danger, man faces the loss of a breathing space for all that is wild and free in his spirit." She had a great sensitivity to this issue, as a woman who had discovered freedom of spirit in exploration, and in the air.

Sometimes my mother found it hard, as many women in the heady days of early aviation found it hard, to be drawn back down to Earth, and into the more conventional concerns attributed to the women of her era. She wrote with disappointment about two women reporters coming up to her just before takeoff on Long Island:

"Oh, Mrs. Lindbergh," said one, "the women of America are so anxious to hear about your clothes."

"And I," said the other, "want to write a little article about your housekeeping in the ship. Where do you put the lunch boxes?"

"I feel depressed, as I generally do when women reporters ask me conventional feminine questions. I feel as they must feel when they are given these questions to ask. I feel slightly insulted. Over in the corner my husband is being asked vital masculine questions, clean-cut steely technicalities or broad abstractions. But I am asked about clothes and lunch boxes."

Now, almost 70 years later, few women reporters would be asking women explorers about clothes and lunch boxes, but at the time, these were the questions they were expected to ask, and she was expected to answer, again and again. What a relief it must have been for her to take to the air!

Whether they are aviators, travel writers, photojournalists, astronauts, research scientists, athletes, or war correspondents, all of the women explorers in the following chapters have chosen, like my mother, in the words of Louise Arner Boyd to "enter another world."

It may be the air, for my mother, or vast space, for Dr. Shannon Lucid, or the oceans, for Dr. Sylvia Earle. It may be another culture, as Yva Momatiuk shared the culture of the Inuit in the Canadian Arctic, and "caught the tail end of a changing world," as she later wrote about that experience. It may be the world of another species, one which primatologist Biruté Galdikas entered in her 30 years of work with the orangutans at Tanjung Puting Reserve, and which Dian Fossey, too, entered, in her own work with mountain gorillas in Rwanda, a long, dedicated study for which Fossey ultimately gave her own life. Or perhaps it is simply the world that exists beyond one's own habits and certainties, almost beyond one's capacities, a world of risk, and possibility, and danger, and self-discovery.

To study these women's lives and adventures, scattered over three centuries, is to celebrate the real accomplishments of individuals, of course. But it is also an opportunity to let our imaginations turn toward the future. What other fields of endeavor, I wonder, can we as contemporary women now open for our daughters and granddaughters, as our mothers and grandmothers so courageously opened the doors of exploration and adventure for us? Wherever we go, as women explorers, we will take with us the legacy of those who have gone before, and we will always travel the dual path, as they did, the outer explorer and the inner explorer moving together, forever, into new worlds. ■

THE CALL
OF THE ARCTIC

LOUISE ARNER BOYD 1887-1972

HELEN THAYER 1937-

"The smaller ice...makes a

crackling sound in warm weather,

occasionally there is a swish against

the shore of waves produced

by the overturning and breaking-up

of some ponderous mass.

Loudest of all...is the boom of a berg

as it splits off from the parent glacier

or the crash of bursting ice as a

mighty berg collapses."

PRECEDING PAGES: *As Helen Thayer trekked forward,*
determined to be the first woman to ski alone to the magnetic North Pole,
she was for 264 miles—inch-by-inch and minute-by-minute—
terrifyingly aware of the polar bears whose territory she was invading
and whose effective trick was hiding in plain sight.

HELEN THAYER

LOUISE ARNER BOYD
1887 – 1972

A S SHE BEGAN to make her way familiarly in a world of ice, Louise Boyd found that she agreed with Vilhjalmur Stefansson, the Arctic explorer who'd once wittily referred to the "misnamed Silent North." To her ears, those uninhabited frozen landscapes to which she returned again and again provided the glorious backdrop for an intricate symphony of sound.

For the first 32 years of her life, Louise Arner Boyd, a San Francisco debutante with a privileged background of governesses and finishing schools and the continual need to put family duties ahead of her own desires, had appeared an improbable candidate ever to set sail for remote polar regions—let alone one day to have an Arctic glacier named for her.

But in 1920, as she was approaching her 33rd birthday, the tragedy of her household finally played itself out with the death of her ailing father, the mining magnate John Franklin Boyd. Surviving his wife by only 12 months, he had poignantly seen both of his sons, Louise's brothers, John, Jr., and Seth, fail to live even past their teens. To his credit, though, the elder Boyd possessed the foresight, before he succumbed, to acquaint Louise with the workings of her wealth, thus preparing her to assume her role as head of the privately held Boyd Investment Company. But, given the long inevitability of her mourning, her changed circumstances presented themselves in the event more as opportunity than loss, and the result was that the orphaned heiress took to her new independence with creative zest and increasing self-confidence.

The somber tone of Maple Lawn, the Boyd estate in San Rafael, on the outskirts of San Francisco, was transformed, too, by a steady stream of weekend visitors and dinner guests, all responding to Boyd's newly revealed gifts as a hostess. Yet, even as she was sharing with friends the pleasures of her domestic luxuries, such as a private swimming pool—quite a novelty in those days—she was starting, it seems, already to set her personal sights far beyond the staid boundaries she'd long had to observe.

Louise Boyd's first trips abroad—her debut on the stage of world travel—were to Europe in 1920 and '21.

Made in the company of a respectable female companion named Sadie Pratt, both these early visits were essentially conventional tourist undertakings, even if in France and Belgium nothing could be considered ordinary about the unlovely World War I-scarred landscapes through which they journeyed, bleak impressions of which Boyd regularly jotted in her diary.

What seems lost to record, however, is just what it was that, following those initial, tamer experiences on the European mainland, brought Boyd to focus her attention on distant points both maritime and northerly and, thus, as we now know, into alignment with her destiny.

No matter the impetus, what counts is that, three years later, this California socialite chose to board a sturdy little sightseeing steamer that cruised to the Norwegian archipelago of Spitsbergen and toured the edge of the polar ice sheet. A child of the Pacific Ocean, from that moment in 1924 on, Louise Boyd was never to be happier, never to feel more at home, than when charting new territory in the brilliant wastes high above the North Atlantic.

"FAR NORTH, HIDDEN BEHIND grim barriers of pack ice, are lands that hold one spellbound. Gigantic imaginary gates, with hinges set in the horizon, seem to guard these lands. Slowly the gates swing open, and one enters another world where men are insignificant amid the awesome immensity of lonely mountains, fjords and glaciers."

This haunting passage opens Boyd's first book, a study written under the auspices of the American Geographical Society and entitled, far less evocatively,

The Fiord Region of East Greenland. It is almost as if, with those simple, poetic, and powerful few sentences (complete with mythic echoes), Boyd was permitting herself the briefest of emotional indulgences. By the time she published it in 1935, she was already a veteran of five trips to her northern paradise—four of them expeditions she personally financed—and her carefully staked-out credibility depended on her ability to generate data and produce scientifically grounded observation, not flights of lyrical fancy.

After her introduction to the region on the Spitsbergen cruise in 1924, Boyd had returned home, intent on organizing for herself a more ambitious trip north. In the summer of 1926, those plans came to fruition. She chartered the Norwegian sealer, the *Hobby*, and was likely the only Arctic explorer of that year, or any other, to head out to sea having stopped first in London to be presented at the court of St. James. (One can be pretty sure that neither George V nor his wife, Queen Mary, imagined that the tall, handsome American woman executing the traditional curtsy before them was en route not to the grand hotels of the continent but to those barren icy islands in the Arctic Ocean known as Franz Josef Land, a place where the polar bears far outnumbered the people.)

Boyd's own main contribution, to which she devotedly applied herself during this and all subsequent voyages, was the photographic documentation of everything she saw. Almost entirely self-taught, she was to prove indefatigable. "My photography of coastal features, in panorama and detail, and of ice conditions was an almost continuous process from either ship or motor dory," she explained proudly, "while I took advantage of every opportunity to carry my cameras up to high ground from which I could get wide and distant views that often afforded an understanding of the topography in no other way so clearly and easily obtained."

(Her thoroughness, in fact, proved in later years to have serious strategic as well as scientific value: during World War II, her extensive library of pictorial material, along with other records, was turned over to the government and its use restricted, while Boyd herself was recruited to work full-time for the war effort.)

Much of the precision camera equipment used by Boyd was cumbersome, requiring a crew of assistants to carry it when ashore. Yet even given the rigors of hauling it up slippery cliffs and over loose boulders, there were dangers beyond the unreliability of the terrain.

"IT IS PERHAPS WORTH WARNING prospective photographers," she dryly notes in her second book, *The Coast of Northeast Greenland*, which describes her expeditions of 1937 and 1938, "of the menace of lone musk ox bulls in certain localities...[charging] in a series of full-speed rushes." Polar bears, on the other hand, "although I have several times come upon their fresh footprints, I have never seen...except on the ice."

That original self-sponsored trip in 1926 was, in part at least, actually a polar bear-hunting expedition, with guns, as well as cameras, being used to shoot them. Boyd, often praised as a "crack shot," had taken up marksmanship as a young girl, and she is reliably said to have been capable of bagging a bear from the deck of a moving boat. Yet as time went on and the killing of polar bears for sport began to fall from favor, Boyd, sensitive to criticism, downplayed the catch of that first summer spent on the *Hobby*. "People are always exaggerating," she tartly told an interviewer in 1963. "For instance, it's not true I shot 19 bears in one day." Nonetheless, accounts of just how many bearskins returned with her party to San Francisco in 1926 vary, with one estimate as high as 29.

The *Hobby* had been at one time the flagship for the Norwegian explorer Roald Amundsen, famed as the first man to reach the South Pole. In the summer of 1928, Louise Boyd, having contracted for her second charter of the vessel, found herself swept up by what she was to call, with terse understatement, "serious happenings in the Arctic." Amundsen, himself on a gallant rescue mission in quest of the crew of a downed Italian dirigible attempting the North Pole, was missing. Now the world was holding its breath and hanging on, excitedly, to every dramatic press bulletin.

For three months and "some 10,000 miles," Boyd and her fellow sailors, joined by three officers of the Royal Norwegian Navy, entered the hunt for the vanished hero. It was, as the *Hobby* ploughed doggedly on, almost like a dog being put on the scent of a former master, and Boyd felt it a privilege, she stated later, to have changed her plans for such a noble cause. Yet though several of the Italians were eventually discovered alive, Amundsen himself had somehow perished in his own effort to reach them.

Reported to have bagged 19 bears in a single day, Louise Arner Boyd stands with a Greenland prize in 1926. However, as she began to sponsor further expeditions to the Arctic region, she grew more sensitive to conservation issues.

For her generous help in the search, however, King Haakon VII of Norway awarded Boyd the Order of St. Olaf, First Class, the first non-Norwegian woman ever to be so honored. Yet, despite this and the varied other distinctions she was to gain over the course of her long life, including the coveted French Legion of Honor and the first honorary membership of the American Polar Society offered to a woman, it's quite likely that what mattered most to Louise Boyd were her inanimate Greenland "namesakes" thousands of miles away: Miss Boyd Land, the Louise Glacier, and the Louise A. Boyd Bank.

Labeled thus by a contemporary Danish geographer wishing to bestow upon Boyd lasting credit for her own early discoveries amid the ice fields, these cartographical tributes were the more priceless for the fact that they took the American "amateur" by surprise. "My first intimations that this land [Miss Boyd Land] had been so designated came in a letter...and on seeing the name on [a] published map," she was to explain later.

Our own earliest knowledge of the areas of Greenland Louise Boyd frequented can be traced to a journal kept by English explorer Henry Hudson in 1607, as he sailed in search of the elusive northeast passage to the Orient. The immense and topographically inhospitable island, lying extensively within the Arctic Circle, but since 1814 belonging to the kingdom of Denmark, is today recognized as the world's largest. From the 17th century on, whaling vessels, primarily of Dutch and Danish origin, plied its treacherous coasts, and the tragedy of shipwrecks there was not uncommon.

Boyd's expeditions to Greenland before the outbreak of World War II took place in 1931, 1933, 1937, and

1938, and for each Louise considered it her "good fortune" to be able to charter the same Norwegian sealer, the *Veslekari*. Built in 1918, it had a 350-horsepower engine, with an average speed of eight knots in good weather; as for personnel, the ratio of Norwegian crew to Boyd's handpicked expedition members was three to one, and among the paid staff was a "mess girl" and a female steward. The ship's salon was fitted out as a library, and a cabin area served as a small darkroom.

PENETRATING THE FORBIDDING MAZE of steep-walled fjords that notch the eastern Greenland coast is possible by boat only in the warmer summer months. Boyd, her appetite merely whetted by her trips of the 1920s, was by 1931 ready to master those "hazardous waters." Yet, despite her growing passion to experience for herself the "extraordinary grandeur and beauty" of Greenland's interior, for this woman who claimed always to powder her nose before appearing on deck, careful planning took precedence. Thus, she chose to regard her hard work in 1931 as "primarily a photographic reconnaissance," paving the way for the "more comprehensive scientific explorations I hoped to accomplish two years later."

It was in '31 that she had her first encounter with Eskimos who, living alongside Danish colonists in settlements at Scoresbysund, a part of the northernmost colony of Greenland's east coast, eagerly kayaked out to meet the *Veslekari*.

Later the same evening the men entertained, dancing and chanting, using tin pans for drums. "No one," she wrote later, "can fail to admire and like these Greenlanders, with their quiet, charming manners, their direct eyes and their faces that smile and radiate kindness."

By 1933, however, she had a more strictly defined mission—to study the "glacial marginal features, particularly in the Franz Josef and King Oscar Fiord area." With the "cordial cooperation and assistance of the American Geographical Society of New York," but using her own money to pay the bills, she set off in the company of a handpicked team of scientists. High points of this trip included a moment at the end of July when Louise was fortunate enough to witness the rare spectacle of an iceberg calving and, also, undoubtedly, the five pounds of caviar with which the team, thanks to their leader's largess, celebrated the Fourth of July at sea.   .

DURING THE PERIOD BETWEEN the Greenland expeditions of 1933 and 1937, Boyd had the honor to be an American delegate to the 1934 International Geographical Congress, held in Warsaw. By now a skilled wielder of cameras, she arrived early in Poland, carting her trusty equipment and intending, as long as she was in the country, to spent the time available to record a "good cross section of Polish rural life." It was a project, she conceded, that came as "somewhat of a departure…after long devotion to photography in the Arctic," but her weeks spend there, too, resulted in another book, *Polish Countrysides: Photographs and Narrative.*

As Boyd headed into the now familiar, always perilous Greenland channels in the summer of 1937, she had aboard the *Veslekari* a new squad of scientific specialists. On her previous voyage, her botanist, suffering from acute appendicitis, had taken emergency leave of the ship. Boyd, a dedicated gardener back home at Maple Lawn, then herself shouldered the task of collecting plant specimens in his stead. This time, with another botanist recruited, as well as the usual geologists and surveyors, she also had invited along a hydrographer, to monitor currents and tides, and a skilled radio technician.

But what mainly marked the 1937 expedition was the daunting amount of ice the *Veslekari* encountered, which clogged the water far earlier in the season than anticipated. Such a circumstance in Arctic seas is never other than ominous, and, in Boyd's vivid phrasing, they were forced to play a "tantalizing game of ice-pack tag...a sort of hide-and-seek with the coast." By the last week in August, the crew was even obliged to set off dynamite charges to free the "pinched" ship. Soon blocked again, however, and fighting the clock—winter is swift and implacable in the polar regions—Boyd and her fellow sailors stayed on deck for a sleepless night after a hundred-mile detour in desperate search of open water.

HOWEVER, WHO COULD DOUBT the heightening effect of such dangerous adventure on Louise Boyd's enthusiasm? Returning the following year, she was more resolute than ever that she and the *Veslekari* penetrate as far north as would constitute a record, and by early August, the ice and weather, to her satisfaction, were turning out to be cooperative. Writing in *The Coast of Northeast Greenland* (a book about the 1937 and '38 trips that for wartime security reasons was only published a decade later), she allowed herself the unusual indulgence of a boast: "To the best of my knowledge, ours was at that time the farthest north landing ever made from a ship on the east coast of Greenland."

The *New York Times* agreed. A little over a month later, there appeared in its pages a photo of Louise, looking impressively no-nonsense in her parka. Then, readers learned from a representative of the American Geographical Society that "Miss Boyd may claim the credit of having gone further north in a ship along the East Greenland shore than any other American...."

She had on that occasion arrived within approximately 800 miles of the North Pole, a destination she'd fantasized about since girlhood. But, in 1955, at the age of 67, this gray-haired Colonial Dame and board member of the San Francisco Symphony Orchestra finally, triumphantly, would make it to the North Pole itself.

"In a moment of silent and reverent awe," she reported of her groundbreaking private charter flight, "the crew and I gave thanks for this priceless sight." They had a cloudless view of infinite ice shimmering 9,000 feet below.

"We crossed the Pole," she went on, "then circled it, flying 'around the world' in a matter of minutes. My Arctic dream had come true."

FOR A WOMAN WHO HAD traveled so far and soared so high, always with a private fortune the means to overcoming the odds set against her, her fate in her final years was, sadly, not what she deserved. When both her money and her health had given out, Louise was forced to rely on the generosity of friends as she passed her last days in a San Francisco nursing home.

It is fitting, though, that not long before she died,

Louise Arner Boyd received word that her faithful old companion, the *Veslekari*, had sunk in the frozen waters off Newfoundland. And at her death, her ashes, as she had requested, were flown north and scattered over the icy eternity of the polar region. ∎

"The feel of wind lashing my body

and face without mercy,

and a savage hunger and thirst

combined to make me dig

into a reservoir of strength....

I dug so deep that I came up

with reserves I never knew I had.

But they were there and

I used every bit of it to push my

weakening body on."

HELEN THAYER
1937 –

THE SORTS OF SURVIVAL TRICKS Helen Thayer picked up while skiing alone to the North Pole in 1988 mostly had to do with the indisputable truth that, in fact, she wasn't alone at all. That is, not if you count the polar bears, the fearsome hosts whose territory she was invading and whose hospitality she had every intention of avoiding. "Polar bears are the most magnificent animals I have ever seen, but just now I hope I never see another one in my life," she wrote in the journal she kept from inside her sleeping bag each night, zipped as it was only halfway for fast escape.

This observation came on day four. She and Charlie, her faithful husky, had crossed at least eight sets of tracks that afternoon.

They had 23 more days to go.

Polar bear fatigue was a luxury she could hardly afford.

FROM AN EARLY AGE, growing up with the complete freedom of her family's 10,000-acre New Zealand farm, Helen had found the record-setting adventures of a fellow countryman inspirational. Sir Edmund Hillary was a Kiwi hero who'd earned the entire world's admiration in 1953 when he became one of the first men to reach the summit of Mount Everest. Then, not content to rest on his laurels, he'd gone on to prove himself again on entirely different terrain. In 1958, his five-man team, traveling by dogsled and snow tractor, was the first successful overland expedition to the South Pole since 1912.

But Hillary, as it also happens, was an old chum of the headmaster of Helen's school, and the young student, an eager acolyte, found herself proud to be introduced to the celebrated explorer when he came through town on a visit. For herself, however, she had already known from an early age the obsessive lure of unique physical challenges.

Having scaled her first 8,000-foot peak with her parents when she was only nine and emerged as a champion discus thrower (her 5'3" height first brought laughter from her coach), Helen Thayer was the kind of person bound to surprise few friends when, on the brink of turning 50, she began to talk about fulfilling a lifelong adventure fantasy. Later compellingly chronicled in a best-selling book,

Polar Dream, her midlife rite of passage took the form of a trek alone on foot—a perilous, exhilarating, and record-making journey—to the elusive magnetic North Pole.

Like Louise Arner Boyd, Thayer's desire to experience the stark beauty and isolation of earth's far northern reaches seemed somehow always to have been embedded in her psyche. And after three decades as an award-winning athlete and climber familiar with some of the world's toughest ascents—in North and South America, New Zealand, Russia, and China—she was more than ready, she felt, to take on, entirely by herself, the approximately 350-mile icy trek.

(One says approximately because, as Thayer explains, the magnetic North Pole actually is a concept of place rather than a fixed destination. It maintains its identity as an anchor for one end of the planet by staying "in constant motion as it travels a daily, jagged, elliptical path in a clockwise direction over a wide area, sometimes moving more than a hundred miles in a single day.")

FOR THE PERIOD THAYER SELECTED to make her attempt —March of 1988—the magnetic North Pole would be located just south of "barren, lonely, windswept, ice-covered" King Christian Island, situated almost 800 miles north of the Arctic Circle in the remote Northwest Territories of Canada. She would begin from the appropriately named Resolute Bay, an Inuit settlement and traditional jumping-off point for polar attempts, from there flying on a DC3 cargo plane a short hop, 57 miles further, to Little Cornwallis Island.

At this point she would take her leave of anything remotely resembling a familiar world, setting out to travel the entire distance, walking and skiing, with only the food and equipment she could pull in her sled.

How does one prepare for such a feat of endurance? Thayer, for many years a resident with her pilot husband, Bill, of the foothills of Washington's Cascade Mountains, had every reason to trust her own skills as a seasoned climber, hiker, and athlete. But, since an important factor would be her ability to pull a heavily packed sled over difficult surfaces and in adverse conditions—she began working to increase her strength with a rigorous weightlifting and kayaking program.

Yet, even the -50°F temperatures, hurricane-force winds, treacherous sea ice, and inevitable Arctic assault that awaited her paled as obstacles when compared to the possibility of a polar bear encounter. In the best case, Helen knew she could hope to find herself regarded by these fearless permanent residents of the territory as merely an interloper; in the worst, she understood she would be prey. That she was a creature in her own way every bit as remarkable as they would never occur to them, and her attempt to be the first woman to solo the North Pole was, one can be sure, a distinction lost on bears.

Yet, after nearly two years of planning, only in the last moments of her departure did Helen finally bow to local Northwest Territories wisdom. What she had repeatedly been told was that her chances for survival would increase immeasurably with even a single Inuit husky at her side. These hardy animals, usually worked in teams, are perfect natural bear alarms, and Thayer, after all would have to sleep sometime. Though convinced that the integrity of her journey meant staying as close as she could to the original plan of going it alone, she still agreed to a compromise, accepting at the last minute just one dog.

Happily, Charlie, the stalwart black husky offered to her for the trip, remained cheerfully unaware of his new partner's initial reservations; not surprisingly, he was to earn his passage many times over in the course of the unpredictable days that followed.

"As I turned once again to ski north, I shut the door on civilization. I knew I would see no other humans for a month. I would be entirely alone in this cold, wind-swept, empty place. But there was no time to think about that."

Helen's plan called for a flexible regimen of walking and skiing: Ease of movement meant sticking to the sea ice which offered the better navigational surface. On that first cloudless day, however, she almost immediately bogged down making any headway at all as she tried to progress along the frozen coastal water. Still, the larger problem, really, was neither the *sastrugi*, the name given to the wave-like ice ridges trapping her skis, nor the -32°F temperature, necessitating a neoprene face mask.

"As I skied I had an eerie feeling of being watched," Thayer has written of her uneasy sensations on that bright morning as she and Charlie, each harnessed to and pulling a loaded sled, took to the hard-packed "road." It was like being haunted in broad daylight. Wondering if her new companion could possibly imagine how unnerved she felt, she even admits to confiding, "Charlie, I have never been so scared in all my life. I'm depending on you to warn me if a bear comes our way."

Carefully scanning the horizon, Helen looked for but could find no readily visible clues signaling the presence of the potentially aggressive mother and cubs she'd been warned were spotted rambling close to her route. There's a reason, she forced herself to joke, giving due credit to nature's preservative palette, "why polar bears are white."

Unfortunately for her peace of mind, her local mentors, before she'd set off, had also stressed to her that her potential adversaries were not just invisible but soundless. "You'll never hear a bear come up behind you; you'll know he's come for you when he pounces, then it's too late," they'd told her.

Yet Thayer had grasped, too, that there could be no real way, ever, to quell her fear, and that her best hope was to shift her terror past paralyzing anxiety into a continual vigilance that would make all the difference to her survival. At night, for example, as she slid into her sleeping bag and knew herself to be utterly vulnerable, relaxing enough to lose consciousness required "a giant emotional hand" temporarily pushing aside her anxiety.

HOW MUCH TIME, SHE KEPT trying not to calculate, would it take a bear to rip through the thin nylon layers of her tent?

For extra protection during the daylight hours, her seven-foot blue fiberglass sled, carrying her tent, foodstuffs, radio, and other necessities, was topped off not just with an orange flare gun but with a loaded Winchester rifle. Like Louise Arner Boyd, Helen Thayer had grown up knowing how to shoot, yet for her part, she also understood that, even as alone as she was, with no backup except Charlie, she would only be resorting to the weapon as a last-ditch option. A wounded polar bear in its rage was, of course, the most fearsome possibility of all.

Thayer, as the Greenland-bound Boyd had done before her, was also planning to make extensive photographic documentation of what she saw, especially of the terrain on the islands—Sherard Osborn, Helena, and King Christian—surrounding the Pole. Moreover, she had also agreed to bring back, for Canadian scientists who'd learned of her expedition to the region, snow samples and temperature data.

Thayer, veteran of many mountains, was now being exposed to a new set of expectations. "When you're climbing," she explains, "there's always that summit. You're seeing it get closer and closer. Here there was only a great white flat glistening jumble of ice as far as the eye can see—then, the next day and the next day and the next, it's the same damned thing again!"

Also, she points out, in the Arctic there's the continual awareness that always water is somewhere beneath one's feet. This realization, she insists, is no small matter. Nine years after her journey to the magnetic North Pole, Helen Thayer, in fact, ventured on a solo expedition 200 miles into the Antarctic in order to celebrate her 60th birthday. "But," she says, "the Antarctic has land under it. That's just a huge psychological difference."

HOWEVER, IN 1988, AS SHE plowed steadily on in the direction of King Christian Island, when she moved, often so did the surface beneath her skis. Sometimes, too, the floating beauty of the landscape unsettled her with its eerie aliveness: In one "forest of icy pinnacles...the only sounds were occasional tired, low groans or a long drawn-out tortured squeak as the edges of the

Even Helen Thayer's neoprene mask became frozen during her expedition to the magnetic North Pole where windchill factors reached -100° F. The protective visor was difficult to remove without tearing away any underlying skin adhering to it.

ice pack pushed past each other." In another, the "desolate, lonely moonscape" was so flat she couldn't tell land from sea ice, and only the creaking and groaning helped her guess where water ended and earth began.

WITH JUST A NEW TESTAMENT TO READ and her daily journal to keep when the day's exertions ended, Helen strove to maintain her energy and spirits in harmony on a diet that included crackers, cashews, walnuts, peanut-butter cups, rice, potato flakes, and granola, along with powdered milk and chocolate. Charlie, meanwhile, was hauling on his own blue plastic child's sled 85 pounds of dry dog food—but, after getting his first-ever taste of chocolate, he much preferred to wait for human treats. And though Charlie, at least, never seemed to tire of the butterfly-shaped, high-fat, whole wheat crackers or peanut-butter cups he piteously begged for, his mistress soon was regarding her daily rations as not just monotonous but disgusting. This was particularly true, she confesses, when she lazily mixed up "lukewarm messes," exhibiting little regard for ingredients.

More crucially, however, Helen's body, even with its padded layerings, had from the very earliest hours on the ice been reacting to the exigencies of the cold in a variety of unpleasant ways. These ranged from simple affronts to her vanity (her eyelashes broke off) to painful and aggravating injuries (she suffered from huge fingertip blood blisters that refused to heal). What must count as her greatest setback, however, came on day 20, as she had arrived a mere two miles from her Polar goal.

"It was at that juncture that a sudden fierce storm unleashed blasts of violent wind and shotgun-pellet-like snow that not only blew away most of her remaining food and fuel but also painfully scratched her eyes with ice particles, swelling her lids and freezing blood from her cuts to her face.

"Panic is not part of me," declares Thayer. "You can't take adverse conditions personally. If the fingers are frostbitten and the eyes are sore, you just go on." Yet, later she was to understand that, as she'd sought shelter from that Arctic onslaught, staring down disaster and mastering the moment, she'd learned an important truth about herself. "It was a big explanation point in my life, really," she now says, "to know that when things got that tough, I was never unhappy. I was up the more the chips were down."

The next morning, day 21—March 20th—brought success. Helen finally arrived at her her long-sought and dreamt-about destination, choosing not to mind that the landscape aspects of the magnetic North Pole rather closely resembled all the other scenery she'd slogged past every other day so far.

"THE SURROUNDING ICE LOOKED NO DIFFERENT from any other, the wind and isolation were the same, but I had fought hard to get there and winning the fight felt good." Setting up her tripod, Helen carefully snapped pictures of herself and Charlie posed before the flags of three nations—the United States, Canada, and New Zealand—recording for history "one of the happiest moments of my life."

And yet there was a new goal now—to make it out of there safely and on to her rendezvous, a point at least seven days' journey away. Traveling by now with almost no food or water and with her eyes still quite severely damaged, Thayer knew she would have to conceal such worry-inducing facts from her base camp at Resolute Bay. Checking in by radio (as she did every evening, the only "safety net" she'd allowed herself), she reported the news of her polar triumph, then went on to fib reassuringly to her listener: "I have about ten days of food and fuel. No problem."

What Helen vividly describes as a "turtle existence" from here on became her reality to a greater extent even than before. "The sled is your shell, always with you. One-half step to the right or left, or even a big wide turn and it's still with you." Plunging ahead with frustrating clumsiness (and having to rely on Charlie now as a seeing-eye dog), she was far too focused on each separate forward motion now to torment herself with any nightmare visions of looming and silent bears. "After five hours we had covered only three miles, a record for slowness. But I thought with some satisfaction that three miles were better than no miles at all."

As she struggled on, Thayer was doling out to herself small morsels of walnut meat, her only remaining nourishment, and drinking melted scraped ice. Experiencing a "savage hunger and thirst," she had not just to call upon her incredible willpower but also to dig into even deeper reserves she'd never known she had. Yet on day 27, as debilitated as she was, she could thrill to the beauty of the view above Cape Halkett, from a promontory she'd reached only after drawing on her final energies to make a 500-foot climb and 4-mile hike. It was from near here she would make her last radio call, to signal the pick-up plane.

"The islands all around me were splendid in the clear morning light. The windswept open sea ice I had traveled both north and south looked boundless and empty beneath the pale blue canopy.... With one last look north across the gleaming white ice that Charlie and I had spent so many days crossing, I turned to leave with a reluctance that surprised me."

HELEN AND BILL THAYER returned to the Pole together in 1992, retracing her footsteps and becoming the first married couple to make the daunting trek. In 1994 they walked 600 miles across the Yukon, and in 1996 they crossed 1,400 miles of the Sahara desert on foot. The cracker-loving Charlie, meanwhile, having never before seen a tree or rain or, for that matter, a flea, took to civilization with gusto and has been a member of the Thayer household ever since he and Helen shared their first remarkable adventure. ■

WHERE THE
AIR IS THIN

FANNY BULLOCK WORKMAN
1859 - 1925

CATHERINE DESTIVELLE
1960 -

"Among the silent glaciers and

peaks of the icy wilderness

on the northern boundary of India,

[I] can understand why the

Men of the Hills should invest these

temples, built by architects

no man can emulate...with the incense

of primitive folk lore."

FANNY BULLOCK WORKMAN
1859 – 1925

ERHAPS THE MOST FAMOUS SNAPSHOT from the album of Fanny Bullock Workman's perpatetic life is the one that reveals her indulging in an act of suffragist propaganda from virtually atop the world. "Votes for Women," the sign declares, held by a proud Fanny for the camera to record—20,000 feet above sea level on the bright surface of a remote Asian glacier.

Yet such publicly proclaimed feminist sentiment proved no check to her intensely competitive nature, even—and most especially—when there were challenges issued by members of her own sex. In fact, this adventure-seeking wife and mother had only four years earlier, in 1908, pitched eagerly into battle with one Annie Smith Peck, a rival American mountaineer. She, it seems, had been bold enough to claim to have exceeded Workman's record for climbing higher than any other woman, an altitude of 22,815 feet, attained by Fanny in 1906 while scaling peaks in Kashmir.

The statement by the offending Smith that she had made it to at least 23,000 feet atop Peru's Mount Huascarán, however, was backed up only by her own testimony. Fanny knew, too, that Smith had carried with her little scientific equipment. Such a lack of even the most minimal supporting data made the temerity her rival exhibited seem even more of an affront.

"Another woman mountain climber claims to have surpassed my height," noted the redoubtable Mrs. Bullock Workman, as she preferred to be known, going on the offensive. Fanny well understood that to claim is one thing, to prove a different matter altogether.

With a record that meant a great deal to her at stake, Fanny intended to settle the matter as decisively as possible. Never doubting that she'd prove her case, she initiated, at her own considerable expense, "a careful triangulation" to be undertaken by an impartial team of expert French geographers. Dispatched to Peru, with a final bill for services mounting to $13,000, the Frenchmen reported back Mount Huascara´n's altitude as only 21,812 feet— 1,003 feet fewer than Fanny had attained. Not only did she triumph over the competition, but her singular accomplishment would continue as a women's climbing record for 28 years to come.

THE TRUTH, HOWEVER, IS THAT FANNY Bullock Workman, a child of privilege, simply wasn't accustomed ever to being denied her due. Her father, Alexander Hamilton Bullock, was both prosperous and distinguished, a politician who served a term as governor of Massachusetts in the years just after the Civil War. Meanwhile, Fanny's mother, Elvira Hazard Bullock, was herself the daughter of a rich Connecticut businessman. With a brother and sister preceding her in the household, Fanny was the baby of the family, educated by tutors at home in Worcester, Massachusetts, and later at a New York finishing school for young ladies. She then was sent for two years' further education in France and Germany, where she gained a taste for cosmopolitan life and the world beyond New England.

Returning to Worcester at the age of 20, she met and two years later, in 1881, married William Hunter Workman, a prominent local physician a dozen years her senior. It was to be a partnership in the best and fullest sense of the word. To the couple was born one child, Rachel, in 1884, and by 1889, after numerous trips to and from Europe, they had expatriated themselves to the continent, making their base in Germany.

Yet, at this stage of what was to be a celebrated mutual career as professional (and daring) world travelers, the Workmans still were more proper than convention-defying in their tastes. They passed their time sightseeing, looking in picture galleries, attending concerts, and, in general, pursuing culture. For example, Fanny, during five consecutive seasons, was able to satisfy her passion for the music of Wagner at Bayreuth, Germany, where the annual festival had been inaugurated only 13 years earlier.

During this period, she also found herself drawn to the newly popular sport of climbing, an activity she had initially sampled back home amid the piney scenery of New Hampshire's White Mountains. One of the earliest women to succeed in ascending Switzerland's famed Matterhorn, Fanny also proved her mettle when she reached the alpine pinnacle of Mont Blanc, Europe's highest mountain. However, her major triumphs as a record-setting female mountaineer remained still in front of her. For the moment—accompanied, as always, by the faithful Dr. Workman—she took up another novel leisure-time pursuit, bicycling.

IT HAD BEEN ONLY IN THE LATE 1880S, following the development of the safety bicycle (as opposed to the high-wheeler) and the invention of the pneumatic tire, that the already contagious fad for cycling had truly started to reach epidemic proportions. As a mode of flexible, independent transport, it quickly captivated both Workmans who, settling their young daughter in a convenient boarding school (where she learned to lead a life quite separate from her parents), soon departed on the

*When climbing, Fanny Bullock Workman chose
a conservatively feminine Victorian costume, refusing to
wear trousers or even a divided skirt.
Walking boots with nails driven manually into the soles
facilitated movemnt on difficult terrain.*

first of their numerous thrill-packed, long-distance bicycle journeys.

From the daily progress of each of these trips, the couple distilled their experience into commercially successful books. Part memoir, part travel guide, these volumes served as bibles for cyclists eager to pedal in their tracks. *Algerian Memories: A Bicycle Tour over the Atlas to the Sahara* (1895) was the one that marked their debut as authors; next came *Sketches A-Wheel in Fin de Siècle Iberia* (1897). But not content to rest on their North African and Spanish laurels, the Workmans had the idea to head east in the final years of the century, pedaling 1,800 miles through Ceylon, 1,500 in Java, Sumatra, Indo-China, and Burma; and a remarkable 14,000 more across India.

Nothing seemed to daunt them, not blistering heat nor violent monsoons, neither bandit attacks nor marauding animals, and the book that resulted from their unprecedented four-wheeled Asian odyssey bears the busy but evocative title, *Through Town and Jungle: Fourteen Thousand Miles A-Wheel Among the Temples and People of the Indian Plain* (1904). Yet the true importance of this already amazing experience comes from the fact that it was merely the curtain-raiser for the more extraordinary dramas that lay ahead.

For, in India, the Workmans had not only glimpsed firsthand the mysterious grandeur of an ancient civilization but, fleeing the merciless heat of the Indian plains for the cool relief of the mountains in 1899, they had also seen for themselves the even more mysterious grandiosity of the mighty Himalaya, India's northern barrier and the tallest mountains on the planet. Swept by their passion for the uncharted, icy fastnesses they glimpsed, they immediately set about making arrangements to return.

To the exploration and mapping of these daunting summits and their perilous valleys, Fanny and William were to devote the next dozen years and thousands of words in five books: *In the Ice World of Himálaya* (1900), *Ice-Bound Heights of the Mustagh* (1908), *Peaks and Glaciers of Nun Kun* (1909), *The Call of the Snowy Hispar* (1910) and, finally, their most acclaimed narrative, *Two Summers in the Ice-Wilds of Eastern Karakoram* (1917).

"The Abode of Snow," they dubbed the region in a poetic litany to its mesmeric power, extolling its "thousand pillared ice halls, the grandly chiselled gopuras, the golden pinnacled *sikras*, that for 1,400 miles on the north, form a dazzling chain of glory, protection and power to India."

Yet its seductively overpowering beauty existed, of course, in exact proportion to its dangers. Alpine veterans that the Workmans were, they felt obliged to point out in the introduction to the first work produced out of their new passion, *In the Ice World of the Himalaya*, that any climb there would always be vastly more taxing and dangerous than a comparable Swiss ascent.

Here is the couple's assessment of the basic difference in the hardship factor: "In the Himalaya, there are no villages and hotels within a few hours' distance of the summits, no shelter huts, where the climber may break the journey and spend a fairly comfortable night, no corps of guides, who in case of need are ready to render assistance."

It hadn't been all that long ago—a mere decade and a half, in fact—when an intrepid Englishman, W. W. Graham, had staged India's first sport climb. But, even after 15 years, it was still a unusual choice of pastime, and certainly never an easy one.

For instance, for purposes of Fanny and William's expeditions, almost all the specialized climbing gear they employed, including their rope, had not been created for the purpose for which it was being used. Improvisation of this sort meant that to achieve slip-resistant hobnailed boots, one simply pounded nails into the soles of stout leather walking shoes. And portable oxygen, for relief at the highest altitudes, was not available.

As for Fanny own climbing garb—never mind her stance on woman's rights—she continued, as she always had, to forego ease of movement with her refusal ever to don trousers or even a divided skirt. She also favored hats, thick scarfs, and protective veils. As the curtain went up on these Himalayan adventures, she was a 40-year-old woman, short of stature, heavily built, and after so many years of vigorous cycling, exceedingly fit.

OVER THE NEXT 13 YEARS Fanny Bullock Workman, with William, was to make the glacial plateaus and treacherous peaks of the Karakoram her proprietary destination. A western mountain range contiguous to the Himalaya, but considered a distinct system and long closed to outsiders, the Karakoram region was India's most desolate and unknown territory and, therefore, to Fanny, its most alluring.

Later, in *Two Summers in the Ice-Wilds of Eastern Karakoram*, she was to put her feeling for the landscape this way: "In spite of hardships and obstacles encountered, [it] was ever tightening its grip on my soul...." Most particularly, there, inside and hidden away, was the challenge of the 46-mile-long Siachen Glacier, the longest, widest, and most inaccessible such formation in Asia.

Among the earliest climbing feats Fanny claimed while laying personal siege to the Karakoram was her attainment of the 21,000-foot-high Mount Koser Gunge, then a record-breaking summit for a woman. And the world beyond India took note, which was only natural since she and William were already, through their travel writing, bona fide media stars. But Fanny, enjoying the fresh adulation aimed at her alone, felt impelled to seek further attention-getting follow-ups and started looking around for other records to set.

Thus, she soon went on to best her own altitude on Mount Lungma; there in the Baltistan region of the Karakoram she summited at 22,568 feet. But it was three years after this success, in 1906, during her ascent of Pinnacle Peak in Kashmir's Nun Kun Massif that she gained the record, 22,815 feet. Although the altitude was corrected, eventually, from her original claim of 23,000 it was still high enough to stand unbeaten for another 28 years.

Finally, in 1912, in what was to be their eighth and final assault on the region, Fanny and William penetrated deep into the eastern Karakoram to survey the Siachen, or Great Rose Glacier. This was an expedition headed by Fanny—she and William alternated acting in that role, switching with each trip—and the mapping activities they undertook were sponsored jointly by the Royal Geographical Society and the Survey of India.

Locating a previously undiscovered pass through the mountains near the Siachen Glacier was just one of the significant accomplishments Fanny had to her credit on this exhausting and exhaustive trip. She was exhilarated, also, to be able to identify a new route across uncharted snowfields to the ice mass of the Kalberg Glacier. (She was less thrilled, though, when mistaken reports of her death from a fall into a crevasse elicited hundreds of premature obituaries in newspapers around the globe.)

The Workmans' serious additions to the geographical knowledge of this massive glacier and its environs brought for the first time genuine respect from their peers. (The publication of *Two Summers in the Ice-Wilds of Eastern Karakoram* had, in fact, been delayed owing to the outbreak of war in Europe, in the autumn of 1914, with the book finally being issued in 1917.) Most scholars and scientists had, prior to the triumphs of the Siachen expedition, tended to view the Massachusetts doctor and his wife as energetic but dismissable, and, above all, self-promoting, in a particularly "American"— vulgar—sort of way.

Now, however, admiration, and some of it not even grudging, was the tone of the hour. The eminent Scandinavian explorer, Sven Hedin, whose own turf was central Asia, commented that *Two Summers in the Ice-Wilds* was "one of the most important contributions ever given to our knowledge of these mountains."

Returning to Europe from India in 1913, Fanny and William set up house in the south of France. Frequently invited to lecture at alpine clubs, learned societies, and other organizations, Fanny was a fellow of the Royal

Geographical Society as well as a corresponding member of the Geographic Society of Washington.

WITH HER LONG HISTORY OF CONTINENTAL school and travel, Fanny spoke French, German, and Italian equally well, and she received honors from or had affiliations with the distinguished geographic societies of France, Germany and Italy. As a proud American abroad, however, she also continued to maintain her standing with the American Alpine Club and the Appalachian Mountain Club of Boston.

Fanny is credited with having been the first American woman asked to deliver a lecture at the Sorbonne in Paris, and she was the second—Isabella Bird Bishop had preceded her—invited to London to address the Royal Geographical Society.

Fanny Bullock Workman died in Cannes in 1925, a scant two weeks after her 66th birthday. She left bequests, most notably, to four women's colleges: Radcliffe, Bryn Mawr, Smith, and Wellesley. Of her conquest of Mount Koser Gunge, more than two decades earlier, she had described part of her purpose in writing about it thusly: "For the benefit of women, who may not have yet ascended above 16,000 feet but are thinking of attempting to do so, I will here give my experiences for what they are worth."

Said her devoted William, concluding a lengthy eulogy, "She was a firm friend and a loyal wife." Traveling alone at last, Fanny's ashes were sent home to Worcester where they were buried in the Rural Cemetery there. ■

"For me, rock has soul."

CATHERINE DESTIVELLE
1960 –

WHEN FRENCH ALPINIST Catherine Destivelle dances, she does so vertically, ascending the mountains she selects as her partners with astounding grace.

As performances, her difficult climbs are self-choreographed ballets of precision and daring. They display athleticism that goes beyond the realm of the highest of high-wire acts. And, as gestures of respect to the far extremities of our planet's grandeur, they combine aspects of both pilgrimage and conquest.

Yet, as breathtaking as Catherine's mountaineering exploits have been—among them, the legendary north face of the Eiger, the 20,470-foot-high Nameless Tower in the Karakoram, and Tibet's Xixabangma, lying to the west of Everest—they not only break records but also give form and force to her own yearnings.

Like so many other adventurers who have listened to that inner call to push past the most dangerous edges of experience, she has had to learn, however, to ignore the distracting clamor brought on by her every triumph.

What's more, public reaction is worked up even to a greater degree of intensity by the media when presented with such a deceptively delicate-looking woman in combination with such a punishing sport. And since she is very pretty, there has always been the need for her to put up with the pin-up brigade or to simply accept that there are those headline writers and photo editors whose jobs require them to define her by her attractiveness first.

"Sometimes I want to be famous, sometimes not," she has confessed. After 15 years in the glare of the transglobal media spotlight, she has heard herself colorfully dubbed the "Rock Queen" or a "Rock Star" and acclaimed as *"la grande dame des sommets."* Because of this, she understands only too well the difficulties of remaining harmoniously focused on one's inviolate goals "when people speak about you in a way that you don't recognize yourself."

THE INTIMATE RELATIONSHIP that Catherine, over two decades, has learned to forge with her mountains, allowing them to reveal their forbidding secrets to her, was not exactly what her parents had in mind when they first encouraged her involvement with a local alpinists club.

All her mother and father had been hoping for, back in 1972, was to identify a suitable outlet for their fearless 12-year-old's racing energies. "I was a dynamic child," she laughs. "I needed to be outdoors and moving around."

Growing up in the southern suburbs of Paris in the mid-1970s, she was soon devoting weekends and holidays to the challenges of her absorbing new activity. "I didn't know I would climb…at the beginning I just wanted to be in the mountains with the cows and the sheep," she has explained.

But her alpine club weekends quickly became more than just playing at Heidi, and whatever simple bucolic satisfactions she'd experienced were supplanted by a more complex feeling of purpose: "I always follow my instincts, and, generally, they are never wrong."

By the time she was 17, Catherine had begun sneaking off on weekends to the mountains in order to keep her more daring climbing plans from her worried parents who, understandably, were now left wondering just what it was they had let themselves in for. Happily for them, though, as soon as she had finished her final lycée year in Paris, Catherine went on to train as a physiotherapist.

With a degree and, soon, a job, her ambitions, for the time being, seemed fulfilled by the steady, thoroughly respectable professional status she had achieved. And though her attachment to climbing was as passionate as ever, it was still, to her, only a recreational pastime.

Fate, however, was waiting in the wings.

One day—just "by chance," Catherine says—an acquaintance asked her to be the featured climber in a film he was working on. At the time, her reputation in the local amateur climbers community, a group of aficionados who regularly ran across one another amid the boulders of Fontainebleau forest, was that she was "fast."

Such speed would be obviously be a boon to anyone shooting a climb on a tight budget. And, of course, there was the fact, too, that she was photogenic.

Quitting her job (though telling her patients she'd return in three months), Catherine was, as it turns out, on the verge of resetting her personal compass altogether.

"NATURE'S MUCH STRONGER than you are, so you have to have a certain humility," she has wisely observed. The importance of Catherine's own strength, however, can never be underestimated. Here, after all, is a woman who has broken her back and kept on climbing, fractured her pelvis and kept on climbing, broken her leg and kept on climbing.

But the experiences that seem so harrowing to others are regarded much more matter-of-factly by Catherine herself. The very first time she suffered a serious accident, in 1985, she was in Chamonix, in the Haute-Savoie, at the foot of Mont Blanc

"I forgot I was walking on a glacier," she says, amused now at the rather basic nature of her oversight, although the resulting fall into a crevasse wasn't funny at all: She'd broken her back.

Struggling out of the 115-foot-deep fissure in the ice with the help of a companion, she immediately returned to the climb, unaware, she states, of the severity of her injury. Soon however, expert medical diagnosis told a different story. Yet barely two months later, she was already up and moving around again, as the mountains once more cast their spell over her.

The same year, curious to see how she'd fare in the controlled atmosphere of a contest, Catherine traveled to Italy where she competed in a newly established international tournament of climbing skills. She took first prize, gaining the highest scores in all three areas of judging—technique, speed, and style.

She would repeat this victory for five straight years.

"The journalists," she comments wryly, "they run after your image. I was embarrassed that first year at the way they saw me. But, then, when I won the next year, I felt better about it."

But by 1991, she had declined to compete any longer—and not just because her success at these events had started to seem to her predictable. "That sort of climbing, in competition, with ropes, is just gymnastics, there's no risk at all. In mountain climbing, there's the *real* adventure."

WITH A WEALTH OF PEAKS in every climate and time zone from which to choose, Catherine has boldly taken the measure of many. Her preference is to follow winter around the globe. She points out, in the season of coldest weather, frozen landscapes offer the fewest surprises.

Thus, in 1992, she made a winter ascent of the Eiger's north face ("the most deadly of the Alps"), and, on the other side of the globe, she scaled the imposing Latok column in Pakistan. And, in 1993, she returned to Switzerland, to the Grandes Jorasses (along with the Eiger and the Cervin, one of the daunting triumvirate of the northern Alps). Then to Asia again, where in Nepal she attempted both Annapurna and the Makalu, the world's fifth highest summit.

However, two of her best known and most thrilling expeditions took place in 1990. It was that year in Pakistan that she made her historic free climb of the Karakoram's Trango, or Nameless Tower, and, in France, she soloed the 660-yard Bonatti column in the Petit Dru region of the Mont Blanc range. Although the classical route on the north face of the Petit Dru had been climbed before, it was the first time that Walter Bonatti's route had ever been solo-climbed since the ascent of the master alpinist himself. But where his route to the top had been a five-day ordeal in 1955, her own assault, as a result of far easier conditions, was an amazing, bare-handed "express" trip of only four hours on the same face.

When, in 1991, she returned to the western wall of the Drus, however, the outcome of her effort was far different. Now she was opening her own route, and, with crippling weather conditions facing her, she was forced to make several bivouacs virtually in midair. It was an 11-day endurance test, 3,000 feet above sea level, earning her loud choruses of admiration for the solitary heroism she evinced. And, in the Alps, the "Destivelle route" was the first rock face ever to bear the name of a woman.

"You have to learn how to read the walls," she has said. "It demands a certain mind-set. You set off when you're feeling good and when you're ready, you just start to climb." According to Catherine, one gets into "a kind of second state [that's] very focused, with no thoughts beyond the climb. You don't even think about reaching the top...just feet, hands...feet, hands."

The self-belay system that she has developed, enabling her to take on nearly any rock face using primarily her hands and feet alone, requires the following: maintaining near-superhuman balance and composure; keeping one's instincts functioning at their deepest, most intuitive levels; and, above all, holding firm to a clear faith in oneself.

Getting the exact right rhythm, too, is crucial. And, as Catherine says, "Up there you need quick reactions."

In 1994, again with the image of Bonatti as her guiding spirit, she followed the route he had opened alone on the north face of the Cervin—also known as the Matterhorn—crowning his career in 1965. It was a "fiendishly difficult" ascension for Catherine, *"une femme fragile,"*—or so said the general press, though they should have known better.

She had bested his time by two days, and now could pronounce herself satisfied, finally having completed the last of the trio of northern Alpine faces. Since Bonatti's day, no climber had even attempted to brave the north side of the Cervin alone.

TRAGEDY WAS AVERTED, but only barely, for Catherine two years later in Antarctica's Ellsworth Land where, with her husband, Erik Decamp, she was attempting to scale a virgin face of the Ellsworth Mountains. (The territory and the range were named for American explorer, and backer of Roald Amundsen, Lincoln Ellsworth, who, in 1936, had accomplished the first flight over the continent.)

"I lost my balance on a slope," recounts Catherine, straightforwardly. "It was at 4,620 yards, and there was no one around, no radio, no [possible] rescue party. It was an open fracture of my leg. I tried to push on, but it was bleeding. For 16 hours, with one rope, we made 27.5-yard rappels...when we reached the tent, a storm [suddenly] woke up, and we were stuck for three days."

IN 1996, WHEN THE 36-YEAR-OLD Catherine was three months pregnant with her first child, she journeyed to Scotland to make a solo ascent of the 450-foot sandstone tower, the Old Man of Hoy. It was an unroped ascent, except for one pitch. Accompanying her, as usual, was Erik, himself a skilled mountain guide and climber besides being his wife's devoted mainstay and, frequently, her creative troubleshooter.

Once, when climbing in Thailand, Catherine had had the unusual pleasure of mounting steep cliff walls amid the nests of rare swallows; at other times during her expeditions, she would often fondly hail birds as her best companions. Here, however, an avian species particular to the Orkneys would prove far less amenable to her charms.

The arctic skua, a predatory sea gull known locally as the bonksie, is an aggressive enough creature that, when one was cheerfully greeted by Catherine as she paused, spread-eagled on the rock face, nearly in sight of her goal, it thought nothing of returning the salute by casually vomiting in her face.

Yet, that inhospitable display was merely insult added to injury, since the storms that had greeted them upon their arrival had almost proved definitively discouraging, with conditions excessively hostile even for such a desolate northern spot. In fact, the general tolerance in that part of the world for violently inclement weather, as shown by the natives, has continued to impress Catherine ever since.

"The Scottish people are amazing. They're outside in all kinds of weather," she said, upon her return in 1998 to climb Scotland's Ben Nevis. She was accompanied this time by her son, young Victor, as well as his father. "[Ben Nevis] is not very high," she admitted. But, possibly, she regarded the trip, anyway, more as a method of initiating her infant son—only starting to climb out of his crib—into the vertical way of life his rock dancer of a *maman* has made her own. ∎

DOWN RIVER

FLORENCE BAKER
1841 – 1916

ARLENE BURNS 1960 –

"My feet became very sore

from marching,

as we had to go sometimes

16 miles through nothing but swamps

two or three feet deep."

FLORENCE BAKER
1841 – 1916

FLORENCE BARBARA MARIA FINNIAN VON SASS—
no one seems ever to have known for certain if
that was her actual name—could have been a
creature straight out of romance: a delicate-seeming,
fair-haired young woman about to be auctioned as
a slave, yet rescued in the nick of time from a
proverbial fate worse than death.

She had been born in 1841 to a family later
massacred during one of the many civil wars in
Eastern Europe. All she could ever recall of that

tragic day when she was orphaned at the age of seven was, "shots, knives, yells, corpses and fire."

Apparently, a kindly person had hidden her from the violent marauders, but, ten years later, less favorite circumstances would deposit her helpless at an Ottoman slave market. Her savior this time a bonafide English gentleman, who admitted later to experiencing *un coup de foudre*, or love at first sight, succeeded in outbidding all the other eager purchasers. Samuel White Baker was the Englishman's name, and, after what some say was the equivalent of one pound in ostrich feathers, he carried the 17-year-old Florence triumphantly away from the Turkish auction block.

"I OWE EVERYTHING TO SAM," Florence Baker was to say over the course of her life. However, she never elaborated further on the highly unusual circumstances under which she had met her future husband.

Samuel Baker chose to maintain an equally discreet silence on the subject. For the footloose 38-year-old widower, whose own children were being cared for by relatives back in England, the new relationship that unexpectedly absorbed him was one he knew would be impossible to explain to polite society or to expose to its judgments.

The only answer, then, was to put a safe distance between themselves and those civilized milieus where disapproval or even ostracism would inevitably be the response.

To this end, Samuel and Florence Baker (courtesy, and his devotion, allowed her to use his name in those years before they were legally married) set sail for Africa, embarking on the tandem career that would eventually earn him a knighthood and guarantee, for her, to use the phrase of an admiring 19th-century historian, "a high place in the story of Africa."

TOGETHER, THE COUPLE HAD COME to Africa intent on pinpointing the location of the Nile's source waters. It was a high-stakes goal that put the wealthy Samuel and Florence in direct competition with a rivalrous assortment of glory-seekers, including the Scot David Livingstone and fellow Englishman John Speke, whose path they would eventually cross. (Samuel, in fact, had earlier been rejected as a member of the Livingstone expedition, its leader dismissing him as a mere dilettante sportsman.)

After setting off from Cairo on April 15, 1861, the two would become veterans of the unceasing hardships that the continent's sinister interior, with its extremes of climate and its warring tribes, offered to even the most experienced travelers. They had crossed the Nubian Desert, enduring temperatures of 110°F in the shade, slaughtered a marauding hyena in their own sleeping tent, and buried at least one member of their party in the desolate Nile swampland. Fortified only by their strength of purpose, Samuel and Florence survived everything from mutinous bearers to malarial waters.

By June of 1862, the Bakers stopped in Khartoum (now the capital of Sudan), a rough-and-tumble town marking the last Nile settlement navigable by boat. Dutch explorer Alexine Tinné's mother, visiting there at the time, wrote in her journal:

"A famous English couple have arrived. Samuel and Florence Baker are going up the Nile to find Speke.

In North Africa, the Bakers traveled in relative luxury unaware of the

They have been traveling to Ethiopia and I hear she has shot an elephant! She wears trousers and gaiters and a belt and a blouse. She goes everywhere he goes."

The Bakers spent six months in the slave-trading town gathering supplies before they began the next 1,000 miles journey, up the Nile, to a remote town called Gondokoro.

Before leaving for the south, they were amazed to encounter fellow explorers John Speke and James Grant, figures whose survival, until that moment, the Bakers had regarded as uncertain. Speke and Grant, for their part, were startled to meet Florence, and they disapproved of Samuel's casual assumption that she would accompany him into ever more dangerous territory. They did not understand how he could put a lady in what they viewed as great jeopardy.

hardships they'd later encounter as they searched for the source of the Nile.

The Bakers, for their part, were discouraged to learn that Speke and Grant had staked their own claim as the first European explorers of Lake Victoria, the principal source of the Nile. However, the couple's spirits were buoyed again once the alluring details of a mysterious second lake, not yet charted, began to be revealed. Speke and Grant, who themselves had been prevented from reaching the lake, took pains to caution their friends about the infamous King Kamrasi, a local ruler who had a habit of offering nasty surprises. However, because this despot held sway over the heart of the territory through which they needed to pass, it would be nearly impossible, they told the Bakers, to avoid him.

Reinvigorated by the idea of the quest for Luta N'Zige, or dead locust, as the lake was known to Africans),

Samuel and Florence began assembling their plans. They could not envision then that they would spend more than a year in the struggle to reach Kamrasi's kingdom, followed by another year to reach the fabled lake.

With ill-wishers around Gondokoro stirring up efforts to deprive them of crucial basic support—the Bakers were reputed to be foreign spies, making them objects of fear and suspicion—it was Florence whose strong will and reasonable arguments most often managed to neutralize the effect of any sabotage. She dealt especially skillfully with one antagonist, a hostile slave trader named Ibrahim. After leaving Gondokoro, they soon found themselves in desperate need of the protective escort that they believed his caravan could provide, yet he was resisting their ploys to force his hand.

Florence finally appealed to him directly as he tried to ride past them, at a time when they were stopped on the road. Though unwillingly, the trader did pause. This slight hesitation provided all the opening Florence and Samuel needed to press their case. Ibrahim had other reasons to respond favorably to Florence: Her kindness to his own daughter, who at times traveled with him, had touched him and led him to become their most important ally. He would often turn up in true cavalry fashion throughout the nightmarish months to come.

Arriving next in the territory of an Obbo chieftain Katchiba (who was father to a reputed 116 offspring and who traveled on the shoulders of a slave), Samuel was surprised to find himself in demand as a deputy rainmaker. And though he and Florence longed to make their escape from Obboland, all of their horses, camels, and donkeys had succumbed to disease, forcing the couple to wait months until Ibrahim could supply them with oxen, beasts whose stately pace was suited to their current state of fatigue.

For, as they had begun to run out of their quinine supplies, they'd quickly started to be plagued by malarial fevers and exhaustion. Matters from then on had gone swiftly downhill: According to one lurid account of their misfortunes, rats ran freely in their tent as they lay too ill to move, while across their bodies crawled armies of white ants. A few servants did stay loyal, but others, increasingly, revealed their true opportunistic colors.

Turning back, however, was never a possibility.

IN JANUARY OF 1864, they were at last ready to head off again. Soon their Obbo bearers—at this stage few in number and sullen in mood—deserted them. Then, Florence was painfully injured when she was thrown from her bullock, while Samuel's own ox had bolted into the bush at the earliest opportunity. Their guide, it was disturbingly obvious, was intentionally leading them miles out of their way.

On January 22, as they came within sight of the cascading Nile again, they were actually a mere 60 miles away from Luta N'Zige. However, lacking any maps of the region, they had no way of knowing just how close they were to realizing their ambition. They pressed on. When, finally, they did enter Kamrasi's territory, the initial ceremony of welcome was a hair-raising mock attack.

BY THE TIME of the Bakers' meeting with the man they believed to be King Kamrasi, (actually a royal brother posing as the monarch) and receipt of permission to proceed to Luta N'Zige, they had become impatient. Still in much less than perfect health, they were caught unaware by the outrageous proposition the king would make before permitting them to press on. Samuel recounts:

"I now requested Kamrasi to allow us to leave, as we had not an hour to lose. In the coolest manner he replied, 'I will send you to the lake and to Shooa, as I have promised; but, *you must leave your wife with me*!'

"At that moment we were surrounded by a great number of natives, and my suspicions of treachery at having been led across the Kafoor River appeared confirmed by this insolent demand. If this were to be the end of the expedition, I resolved that it should also be the end of Kamrasi, and, drawing my revolver quietly, I held it within two feet of his chest, and looking at him with undisguised contempt, I told him that if I touched the trigger, not all his men could save him: and that if he dared to repeat the insult I would shoot him on the spot."

Florence Baker, the woman at the center of this duel of wills, was seated nearby, watching closely. Samuel Baker was ready to kill to protect her, yet Florence also knew how to hold her own ground. Frequently dressed for comfort in trousers, gaiters, and rough boots, she had fought next to Sam when attackers threatened, efficiently loading ammunition. She had also hunted big game by his side, dining on chewy hippo washed down by champagne.

Thus, on that tense occasion when the king appeared to be claiming her for himself, she reacted aggressively mere seconds after Samuel did:

"My wife, naturally indignant, had risen from her seat…, she made [Kamrasi] a little speech in Arabic (not a word of which he understood), with a countenance of Medusa…. Whether this little *coup de théâtre* had so impressed Kamrasi with British female independence that he wished to be off his bargain, I cannot say, but with an air of complete astonishment, he said…'It is my custom to give my visitors pretty wives, and I thought you might exchange…. I will never mention it again.'"

MORE EAGER THAN EVER TO BE MAKING progress, and to put some distance between them and "Kamrasi," they hastened away. They were unaware that, incognito, the genuine king had been one of the noisy crowd following behind, keeping his own watchful eye on their actions.

Then, out of the blue, while fording the Kafoor River, crossing on top of dense weeds that barely supported their weight, Florence suddenly stopped moving.

Worse still, though Samuel saw his devoted companion freeze in paralysis, he could not reach her quickly. He watched in horror as she pitched forward, sinking like a stone through the thick green carpeting. Frantically, Sam finally reached her. Had she drowned? It seemed to be the case, and he even believed he'd heard a death rattle signaling the end.

In fact, felled by sunstroke, Florence was for ten days comatose then delirious. At times she so much resembled a corpse that her despairing husband actually went so far as to order a grave dug in readiness.

Her recovery, when it finally came, however, turned out to be closely timed with another cause for jubilation: Only one day's march from her "deathbed," the Bakers reached the western shore of Luta N'Zige.

"It is impossible," Samuel later wrote, "to describe the triumph of that moment—here was the reward for all our labor—for the years of tenacity with which we had toiled through Africa…. I looked down…upon that vast reservoir which nourished Egypt and brought fertility where all was wilderness…. As an imperishable memorial of one loved and mourned by our gracious Queen…I called this great lake the 'Albert Nyanza.' The Victoria and the Albert Lakes are the two sources of the Nile."

Florence, though still weak, leaned proudly on her husband's arm as they descended a steep cliff of 1,500 feet to the edge of the water. Overcome by the moment, Samuel left her side and plunged impulsively into the waves sweeping before them, while Florence fixed a hair ribbon to a bush by the lake's edge.

Enchanted by the natural splendor of their new surroundings, they soon were making plans to explore Albert in a large, single-log canoe that had a cabin built-on. During this excursion, they marveled at the lush meadows that gave way to waterfalls cascading down sheer granite walls, at the spectacle of elephants spraying one another, at the lazy ease of hippos floating past.

But Lake Albert also presented the hazards of extreme weather, and they quickly grew to expect the onset of a violent storm in the middle of each day. Its gales were strong enough to create waves that could swamp their vessel, putting it in danger of capsizing. One afternoon, in fact, they only barely made it to the safety of the beach before the craft overturned.

AFTER A HARROWING TREK OUT of Africa, the Bakers made their way slowly back to London. The scandal of their irregular union had preceded them, and though they married in 1865, Queen Victoria continued to refuse to receive Florence at court. The fact that Samuel accepted a knighthood, however, did elevate his wife to the status of Lady Florence. And when he came to write his account of their early adventures together, he was unstinting in his praise of her:

"Had I really come from the Nile Sources? It was no dream. A witness sat before me; a face still young, but bronzed like an Arab with years of exposure to a burning sun; haggard and worn with toil and sickness and shaded with cares, happily now passed; the devoted companion of my pilgrimage to whom I owed success and life—my wife."

The Bakers were to spend three more years in further African exploits, from 1870-73. This time, however, they went at the head of a large, well-armed expeditionary force organized to settle old business. In addition to helping wrest Bunyoro from the control of Kamrasi's successor, Sir Samuel Baker was on a crusade to end the flourishing white slave trade in Sudan.

Sadly, neither mission succeeded. Florence would write later to one of her stepdaughters describing their harrowing retreat, "My darling child, it is quite impossible to tell you about our weary march—I can only tell you that the entire population lay in ambuscades, and we had to fight for seven days through that dreadful country, where it was quite impossible to see the enemy...only showers of spears passed our faces."

She would never return to Africa. In fact, she flatly refused, having had enough, and her husband honored her wishes. They did travel, though, to other exotic destinations, among them Japan and India. Living peacefully in an elegant manor house in the English countryside, Florence survived Samuel by 23 years. And not until many years after her own death did her full role in their thrillingly collaborative history become known to the greater world. ■

"The river speaks in subtle whispers,

and encourages impeccability

in people's actions."

ARLENE BURNS
1960 –

"I WANTED TO GO somewhere where I didn't know anything or anybody in order to learn who I was. I wanted to plop myself in the unknown and see if I would sink or swim. So I bought a one-way ticket to New Zealand and left with 600 bucks in my pocket."

"And what I found was how little I knew, and how curious I was to learn more."

Calling herself a "freelance adventurer," outdoorswoman Arlene Burns has carved out a colorful career pitting her skills against the elements and learning on the go in what are often extreme situations.

According to her own tally, she has journeyed by elephant, horse, camel, mountain bike, tractor, train, truck, rickshaw, tank, kayak, fishing boat, yacht, hang glider, sailplane, airbus, local bus, balloon, buggy, and foot. Yet whether scaling remote Russian volcanoes, navigating forbidden Tibetan rivers, galloping across Mongolia astride a "half-wild horse," or making the acquaintance of a Costa Rican tarantula, she recognizes how her "extraordinary adventures [have caused her to] pay attention and question."

"Traveling does for the mind what exercise does for the physical body," she likes to say. "One has to be open to the unfamiliar and not be intimidated by it."

And every time Arlene narrowly escapes death in the course of pursuing the strenuously active life that sustains her, she adds another chapter to her personal legend. It's a small number of people, after all, who can cheerfully claim, as she does, "Many times I've been a fingernail sliver away from being flat-as-a-pancake dead! Once, for example, I'd contracted meningitis after my friends and I had spent several days carrying our kayaks upstream on the Marsyandi River in Nepal.

"I knew I was really sick, as my neck was stiff, and my head felt like it would explode through my skull. I had a fever of about 105°F and could feel my brain frying. I was hallucinating, totally wiped out and lying on the shore of the river. I intuitively knew I had meningitis, and wondered if I would die soon."

But, sensing the simple power emanating from the natural world around her—"the birds chirping and the river dancing by," it came to her that "dying on this sandy beach was much better than dying in a third world hospital."

Soon, however, because they lacked the supplies to linger there any longer, Arlene and her companions were forced to pack up and get in their kayaks once again. "I had no excess energy to even take an extra paddling stroke, and, then, something happened that changed everything. I began truly to connect to the energy of the river and used very little of my own. I was still burning with fever and hallucinating, but I was paddling in complete flow...when I felt my body overcome the fever, I felt that I had just been reborn."

Stories like these, for all that they enhance her reputation as a dauntless heroine of awe-inspiring, all-weather adventures, offer something beyond their mere temporal value. (Her celebrity status saw her selected to train actress Meryl Streep for an Arlene Burns-type role in the film *The River Wild.*) For her, Arlene says, each of these many brushes with her own mortality has broadened her perspective and deepened her understanding of her "small place in the bigger picture of life."

SIX MONTHS AFTER LEAVING the University of South Carolina in 1980 with a never-to-be-used degree in geology, she was en route to New Zealand with a one-way ticket. She had been hired sight unseen as a whitewater guide on the basis of her stateside experience. It was only upon arriving there, however, that Arlene realized her new employers had been expecting quite a different sort of figure.

After managing, with no small amount of trouble, to secure a work permit for what they'd pictured as a usefully brawny fellow named Burns, the New Zealand team was faced with the startling reality of a blonde, blue-eyed, freckled "Sheila" (local slang for a female) in their midst—and one who stood only five feet, seven inches tall, besides.

"A very common name for a man in New Zealand and Australia is Arlin," she explains, recalling the initial confusion. "So they just assumed I was a guy."

Yet once she started earning her keep—not even given a paddle straight off, she had to earn one—Arlene then spent two years working the New Zealand rivers. She says now that she never ceased to be astounded at the daredevil, broncobusting attitudes common to her male peers there. In fact, shuddering at their casual attitude toward basic water-safety principles, she describes her early days rafting such New Zealand waters as the Wairoa and the Rangitata Rivers as time spent in "the wild west of the whitewater frontier."

By the second season she was manager of South Island Operations, where her duties included training the male river guides. And while the doubting bosses who'd inadvertently brought her over there may have finally started to recognize her value by that juncture, Arlene herself felt "a strong voice whispering from the heart to go see the world." By 1984, she was ready to push on to New Caledonia, Australia, Indonesia, and finally Nepal.

Nonetheless, having been the first woman to work as a whitewater guide in New Zealand, Arlene left behind a door propped open for others. "In general, women trying to break into traditional male occupations end up having to be twice as good in order to be thought of as being half as good. But that's ok in the long run.... Perhaps there is more freedom when people expect absolutely nothing of you."

REMEMBERING HER CHILDHOOD growing up in Columbia, South Carolina, in the 1960s, Arlene Burns unhesitatingly labels herself a "misfit." Often at odds with her divorced mother who would have preferred a more typically feminine daughter, she started instinctively to rebel at a young age. "I wanted to play kickball with the boys, not hopscotch with the girls," she says. "And I loved to ride the family horse that bucked everyone else off."

The world beyond her backyard continually beckoned. "I always wanted to know where the trains were going!" is how she puts it. Thus, Thor Heyerdahl's ocean-rafting memoir, *Kon-Tiki*, was one particularly thrilling book that left a long- lasting impression, and she can even summon up a clear sense of the visceral excitement she felt the first time she studied the map of Asia.

"There was a blue streak, the Brahmaputra River, across the yellow Tibetan plateau, and [she can't help adding proudly] 15 years later, I was on it!"

At the age of 14, determined to separate herself from household conflicts and precociously establish her independence, Arlene took the defiant step, one evening after dinner, of gathering up her sleeping bag and creating a bedroom for herself in the woods near her school. She built a makeshift shelter out of scrap lumber she'd scavenged. Mowing lawns to support herself, she maintained an uneasy truce with her mother and somehow managed to avoid placement in a foster home.

STILL, THERE WAS ALWAYS ONE CONSTANT ELEMENT, one overridingly satisfying aspect of her life from which she took strength and which never disappointed her—and that was the eternally mysterious and alluring wilderness. "It was my church," she states simply, recalling how, above all other relationships, she preferred her increasing communion with the natural world.

In fact, ace outdoorswoman Arlene Burns nearly drowned on her very first kayaking trip, one taken on the black waters of the nearby Edisto River. It was, of course, a fitting baptism for someone whose future was to encompass so many survival tales: "We tried to go over a fallen tree trunk because we didn't know any better and I got pinned in the tree branches with just my nose out of the water. Nobody could get to me. Finally a high school football player, who was with us on the trip, abandoned his kayak and jumped in to save me. I got pretty sick from all the water I took in."

It wasn't until three years later, when Arlene was 17, that she had a chance to attempt kayaking again. In the meantime: "I missed my debutante party for a rock-climbing outing in the mountains," she claims.

THROUGHOUT HER COLLEGE YEARS, Arlene chose, when she could, to spend contemplative holidays back-packing alone through the Great Smoky Mountains, along the North Carolina-Tennessee border. Already, at 18, she had begun to lead wilderness groups, working as a guide in the Boundary Waters of northern Minnesota. "It was the first time I was out of the South and the first time I'd been given a huge amount of professional responsibility."

Included among those tenderfeet she helped introduce to the arduous joys of portage was a group of less than enthusiastic members of the Minnesota Vikings football team: "To portage," she says, "you yoke a canoe on your shoulders, put a big pack on your back and on your front, and walk through the mud swatting mosquitoes and pulling leeches off your legs."

The athletes, it seems, despite long familiarity with brutal training sessions, yearned for more recognizable forms of physical punishment. Faced with perhaps just a bit more of the outdoors than they'd bargained for, "they called it pain therapy," says Arlene.

In her first years as a wilderness guide, it was, Arlene believes, her unswerving confidence that propelled her forward and established her so quickly near the top in such a masculine universe. "I've never had a fear of failure," she states frankly.

Yet, the humility—or, possibly, the humanity—that she always feels comfortable expressing must have played a large part, as well: "I wanted to connect with even the tiniest ounce of commonality in people's lives. I asked questions. I was willing to try. If you try something and you're not afraid to fail, then you usually figure it out and can even find yourself *dancing*."

For Arlene, who for many years has considered herself "as much a Buddhist as anything else," the idea of "dancing" refers to the harmonious interplay between those elements that comprise the basis of any chosen activity. In the case of rafting or kayaking, one recognizes an essential triumvirate comprising the paddler, the craft, and the water.

"It's a graceful, delicate relationship rather than one that's about strength or conquest." Which is to say, in this endeavor, a partnership, not a competition, is the ideal.

THE RECURRING THEME of her own seeming indestructibility is one that can, at times, make Arlene Burns seem nearly a figure out of a folktale, Pecos Pete or Paul Bunyan, perhaps. And, yet, as excessively stalwart as they were, such fabled heroes were surmounting obstacles and carving out their outrageous triumphs on native soil.

Yet her medical chart alone is a catalog of pain and disease endured and triumphed over in every time zone.

For example, as she was snorkeling in the waters off Bali, even the agonizing results of an inadvertent plunge into a nest of stinging sea lice failed to slow her down. Or, in Siberia, trying to kayak despite the excruciating discomfort of second-degree burns on her foot, Arlene permitted herself to be treated with a folk remedy that was as surprising as it was curative: "A man, whom despite the language barrier I determined was a doctor of sorts, applied a black, tarry substance called *momyo*, which is a miracle drug for the Russians. Basically, *momyo* is mouse feces. They collect it in the crevices in alpine cliffs…. He spread the *momyo* on my severely infected burns. It was the greatest act of trust. Imagine letting a stranger put mouse feces on a septic wound!"

She even found her own remedy for the head injuries that impaired her balance after a 1,000-foot fall from an Alaskan glacier. "Months after the fall, I got so frustrated at feeling dizzy that I was determined to fix it. I started running in the rocky riverbeds of the Saluda River in Columbia when the dam wasn't releasing water, to make myself find balance on the loose rocks. It worked, although I skinned my knees plenty in the process."

ARLENE HAD BEEN TANTALIZED since her first

TIM JEWETT

One of her local white-water runs,
Arlene Burns paddles Husum Falls, a ten-foot vertical
drop on Washington's White Salmon River.

glimpse of Tibet's largely unexplored Brahmaputra River in an atlas by its unimaginably distant reality. She also knew that the Chinese government—well aware of the increasing scarcity of such virgin rivers—was asking the extortionate fee of $500,000 to grant permission for the first white-water descent.

Living in Nepal during 1989, she nonetheless remained convinced she could devise a route that would circumvent the authorities and bring her closer to that longed-for river that had haunted her childhood dreams. But before it was all over, however, she, along with her companion and their 200-pounds of gear (consisting of "boats, sleeping bags, a tent, warm clothes, first aid kit, stove, pot, and food, food, food,") would have been temporarily abandoned on a patch of mountain tundra by an unreliable convoy of Chinese geologists, sheltered by friendly Buddhist monks after crossing a sacred lake in a violent blizzard, and nearly held for ransom by Chinese soldiers.

Frozen hands, scorched skin, and a steady diet of *tsampa*, a Tibetan staple of roasted barley flour, were among the least of her travails. Only after losing hope— after 38 days of wandering the often roadless Tibetan interior—did Arlene finally find herself poised on the Brahmaputra's banks, ready to slide in her kayak and "dance" its waters.

"Drifting and paddling in a state of weariness and bliss, we moved in a smooth, steady flow," she writes. "Our boats were transformed from cumbersome cargo into precision 'river-Porsches.'" Curious villagers ran along the Brahmaputra's banks, fascinated at the sight of the two unknown paddlers in such strange boats. From inside her snug plastic craft looking out, Arlene felt an almost transcendent serenity. The landscape seemed to subtly shift around her: What had before felt hostile now appeared benevolent.

"I began to understand the Tibetans' harmony with their environment and the peacefulness of their timeless world. Their strength and gentleness flowed through me, invigorating me, leading me into another dimension. This was the gift of the Brahmaputra, of the hardships and the isolation."

After slipping through the river's currents for a soul-satisfying hundred miles, Arlene Burns returned to land and made her way alone back to Katmandu and on to Bangkok where she swapped her battered kayak for a mountain bike. She then cycled from Bangkok down the Malay Peninsula to Singapore. (In the years since then, she claims she has, on the same bike, covered roughly 4,000 miles of territory around the world.)

LIVING AS INTENSELY as she does, Arlene Burns understands that "travel can become an addiction." She knows, too, that she's been spoiled by doing "these explorations in places where nature is pristine."

"For me, a river is a perfect metaphor for life. It's constantly changing; if it stops, it dies…. And a river doesn't move in a linear way—it moves and meanders and twirls in circles sometimes." What's more, a river "teaches you balance and humility. Perhaps that's why river people the world over are generally so helpful and compassionate."

And remember, she points out, laughing, "Water can fall 10,000 feet and never get hurt." ■

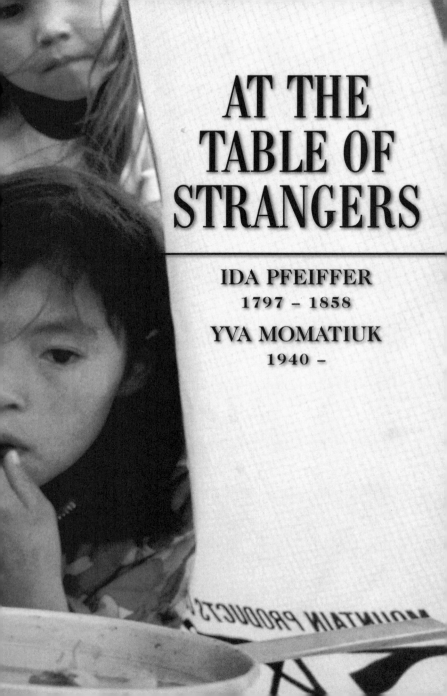

AT THE TABLE OF STRANGERS

IDA PFEIFFER
1797 – 1858

YVA MOMATIUK
1940 –

"There had been so much to see all the way, and every object that met my eyes, even the most seemingly insignificant, had such interest for me that I really forgot my toils, though I did sometimes admire the iron strength of my own constitution that could enable me to get through them."

IDA PFEIFFER
1797 - 1858

T O READ ABOUT THE EXPLOITS of Ida Pfeiffer is to marvel at the sheer force of her determination. After all, in the first half of the 19th-century, transforming herself as she did from a conventional Austrian housewife into a fiercely independent globe-trotter meant being abroad in a world where often the most startling sight on the horizon was Ida herself.

Surviving by her wits alone and enjoying every instant of her often hair-raising adventures, not only did

Pfeiffer once live with cannibals, she even, while sojourning in their midst, narrowly escaped being served up for dinner.

HER CHILDHOOD HAD BEEN AN unusual one. Born in Vienna and raised with a large brood of brothers, Ida Reyer was treated by her father simply as if she were another son. Dressed in boys' clothing and encouraged to excel at outdoor activities, she hardly knew she was a girl at all until the death of Herr Reyer, at which time her mother began attempting, with little immediate success, to put her lone female child into skirts and aprons.

It wasn't long, though, before Ida discovered a new, even more effective way to rebel. She was 17 when she and her mother quarreled over Ida's revelation that she was in love with her tutor. The subsequent household stalemate only came to an end five years later when Ida finally agreed to renounce him.

However much she still pined for her abandoned lover, Ida craved escape from her mother's supervision even more passionately. To this end she agreed to be betrothed to Dr. Pfeiffer, an older widower whose main attraction lay in the fact that he made his home a hundred miles away. Settling into her new life in Lemberg, a city nestled in the northern foothills of the Carpathian Mountains, Ida gave birth to two sons in quick succession. Unfortunately, her husband's career as a lawyer and public official was never to be entirely secure, forcing the plucky Ida to rise to the challenge of maintaining the family's stability.

Nothing about her domestic life in this blighted era was easy. Later, she was to recall vividly her struggles: "I performed household drudgery and endured cold and hunger; I worked secretly for money and gave lessons in drawing and music; and yet, in spite of all my exertions, there were many days when I could hardly put anything but dry bread before my children for their dinner.... I might certainly have applied to my mother or my brothers for relief, but my pride revolted against such a course."

The years passed, and her circumstances changed for the better only when her mother died. Her share of the estate enabled Ida to return to Vienna, leaving the elderly Dr. Pfeiffer behind. Finally, in 1842, as the burden of providing for her sons' education eased, she seized the opportunity to imagine a new life for herself.

As a 45-year-old, middle-class woman making her home in the highly bourgeois milieu of the Austrian capital, Ida's inspiration for what to do next not only was admirably unconventional, it was also totally unprecedented.

It seems that she had always desired—passionately— to travel. "From my earliest childhood I have had an intense longing to go forth into the wide world," she explained. What's more, she meant to do it alone.

Her circle of acquaintances, understandably, was horrified at the very thought. "Men," they said, "were obliged gravely to consider if they had physical strength to endure the fatigues of such a journey, and strength of mind bravely to face the dangers of the plague, the climate, the attacks of insects, bad diet, and to think of a woman's venturing alone, without protection of any kind, into the wide world, across sea and mountain and plain—it was quite preposterous."

Still, Ida remained resolute, or, as she put it, "I had nothing to advance in opposition to all this but my firm unchanging determination." Although she cautiously set her affairs fully in order beforehand and made a will, Ida still felt that divine providence was with her. So it is fitting that for her maiden voyage she chose the Holy Land.

As she waited to board the Danube steamer for the first stage of her journey, Ida was gratified that a contingent of friends and relations had come to see her off. Still, their parting struck her as "bitter," and the underlying tone of the occasion seemed funereal. It was all too clear that the general expectation among them held her survival to be unlikely.

And, in fact, only a week later, while docked at the free port of Galatz, "the place of rendezvous for merchants and travelers from two quarters of the globe, Europe and Asia," Ida received her first intimation of the very real dangers that lay ahead. Because of the elaborate precautions mounted against plague in this teeming border city, a traveler's journey home-

Stubbornly refusing to be discouraged by well-meaning friends who were shocked by her wanderlust, 45-year-old Ida Pfeiffer not only

ward could be rudely diverted if officials suspected even the slightest exposure anywhere along his route.

Professing herself "highly entertained" by the spectacle of the strict separation of outbound and incoming passengers on the docks—a ritual she watched from the safety of her ship's deck—Ida understood that she, too, would be forced to submit to the same protocols if she ever saw Galatz again.

Beset by terrible seasickness as she headed into the Black Sea, she nonetheless fought back the insistent discomfort in order to quit her cabin and experience firsthand "that grandest of nature's phenomena—a storm at sea." Again, her will power, abetted by her toughness, prevailed: "Holding tightly on, I bade defiance to the waves, which broke over the ship and wetted me all over, as though to cool my feverish heat."

rode a camel across the sands of the Egyptian desert in 1842, but also she climbed the pyramids and bathed in the Jordan River.

IN TURKEY, PFEIFFER OBSERVED WITH fascination the harem-like atmosphere of the women's garden outside the mosque in Constantinople. And in the sanctuary she was entertained by the exertions of a dozen dancing dervishes.

Moving on to Jerusalem and then Cairo, still in 1842, Ida along the way mastered the art of camel-riding. She bathed in the waters of the Jordan River, lost her bearings in the mazy lanes of the bazaar at Beyrout, and sturdily climbed the pyramids, turning as brown in the hot desert sun as any "descendants of the Bedouins."

Then there was the night in Egypt when her chamber walls came alive with black bugs. Increasing her misery as she fled to the entrance hall were clouds of gnats that tormented her as she made a second attempt to fall asleep, this time on the cold stones.

As an example of Ida Pfeiffer's fortitude and resilience, it is worth noting that for her even these extreme discomforts could sometimes be seen to have a silver lining. "An additional inducement to rising early" is how she described this last episode, pointing out briskly that "long before sunrise I was ready to continue my journey."

Though pleasing only herself and never intending to contribute to the world's travel literature, Ida did keep a fairly detailed journal. By 1846, four years after her return, a persistent publisher who'd gotten wind of her unconventional odyssey finally succeeded in overcoming Ida's reluctance to go public. The resulting book, *Visit to the Holy Land, Egypt and Italy*, validated his commercial instincts by proving popular enough to require four printings. But, most importantly, the initial payment she received was enough to enable Ida to begin preparations for a next intrepid foray into that great "wide world" awaiting her.

Pfeiffer's second itinerary took as its centerpiece the remote and then little-explored island of Iceland. Today the westernmost state of Europe (and the possible inspiration for the famed Ultima Thule, or end of the Earth, as designated by the ancients), Iceland in the mid-19th century was a bleak, isolated territory long bedeviled by marauding pirates. It was also prone to the ravages of epidemics and volcanic eruptions.

This time a confident veteran both as traveler and author, Ida set out for Iceland with "real ecstasy." She was especially looking forward to being able to "behold nature under an aspect entirely new and peculiar," given such extreme topography as the landscape presented.

But after six months of adopting the simple lifestyle of the native Icelander, she was a good deal less ecstatic: She adjudged the standards of hygiene wanting, the citizens boorish, the culture dull, and the cuisine monotonous.

In fact though, Ida could say "privations and discomforts had no terrors for me," to her, she was never to be an unopinionated—or uncritical—traveler. And it possibly may have been her unenthusiastic reaction to Iceland's Arctic ambiance that helped dictate tropical Brazil as the country she chose to visit.

Conveying Ida, one of just eight passengers (four cabin-class, four steerage), to Rio de Janeiro in the summer of 1846 was the little Danish brig *Caroline*. Yet Rio was only the first port of call on what would be a 19-month voyage circling the globe. Logging 35,000 miles by sea and 2,800 by land, she would avidly soak up local culture as she passed through Chile, Tahiti, China, Ceylon, India, Mesopotamia and Persia (today, Iraq and Iran), and Russia, among other exotic destinations. She was 52 years old and, more than ever, "supernaturally happy" to be finding fulfillment in this itinerant manner.

Her stay in Brazil offered Ida Pfeiffer a first real experience of life in the wild with indigenous peoples. Arriving with her guide at a small encampment of Puri Indians—her journey into the interior had meant slashing for eight hours "through an almost impenetrable thicket"—she was exhausted enough to accept an invitation to spend the night. But before making her bed on the ground, with a cloak for her blanket and a "clump of wood for a pillow," she sat down with her hosts for a meal of roast monkey and parrot. (She had earlier accompanied them on the hunt for this dinner, as well.)

"My appetite was boundless, for I had eaten nothing since the morning," she recalled in *A Lady's Voyage Round the World* (1850). "So I began at once with the monkey and found it excellent; the parrot was not quite so tender and savoury."

Pfeiffer was often introduced by her boastful guide as "a woman of astonishing learning." Thus, she found herself faced with a considerable number of patients hoping her knowledge ran to useful medical advice. But the highlight of her visit to the rain forest was the sequence of dances she witnessed in front of a blazing campfire, its eerie glow accentuating both the beauty and the menace of the performance.

With her nerve endings already ajangle from the ferocious energies of the dancing, Ida realized as she tried to sleep that her mind had become suddenly prey to every sort of fear. What serpents or wild beasts might be advancing upon her as she lay there unprotected on the ground, she wondered with increasing anxiety.

"I rested my head on the log of wood," she tells us, "and consoled myself with the thought that there could hardly be so much danger as travellers would make us believe, or these savages would not sleep so composedly in their open huts, and without the smallest preparation for defensce."

Such sheer sensibleness, as evidenced on this and many other occasions, is the more wonderful for its absolute originality. Ida Pfeiffer was, after all, inventing as she went along a style of life lacking any useful role models, let alone one of her own sex, class, upbringing, age, or nationality. It is only when she later writes disapprovingly of the casual sexuality of the "native beauties" in Tahiti that one remembers her 18th-century origins and 19th-century standards.

However, with the publication of *A Lady's Voyage*, Ida's eccentricities, as well as her crotchets, turned into part and parcel of her increasing celebrity. In fact, so well known did she become that readers around the world eagerly started inviting her to stop with them as she passed their way. Yet money to fund her wanderlust continued a definite problem—even as railway and steamship companies shrewdly began vying to transport her for free and admiring supporters began circulating appeals for contributions to help sustain her.

Then, in 1852, the Austrian government officially recognizing her accomplishments, offered Ida a grant of 150 florins—not a large sum but one sufficient to enable a woman already accustomed to making every economy—to start planning her next trip.

Setting off on her second journey around the world in 1851 Ida sailed from London for Cape Town, intending to investigate Africa. However, she changed plans suddenly and headed East to Singapore.

Alighting finally on Borneo, she soon made, as she had in Brazil, for the interior, forsaking the "heat and morasses" of Pontianah. There, she delighted in regularly crossing the Equator, only a mile away, on foot. And for fully half a year, Ida explored Borneo's least welcoming regions.

Just as she had in her childhood, Ida felt comfortable in men's clothes. For safety, traveling in China five years earlier, she'd passed as a man while wandering through the native quarters of Canton. Now, penetrating the remote territory where the native Dyak tribes engaged in ritual headhunting on the island of Borneo, Ida wore both trousers and petticoats for layered protection and kept on her head a wide bamboo hat, noting, in contrast, that the Dyak women wore "only one garment, and the children, none."

The Dyaks expertly hunted with blowguns and poison darts, and in one of their longhouse settlements Ida had the shock of encountering a gruesome display of enemy heads. Even as she recoiled from the loathsome sight, she could not help philosophizing, "[Are] we Europeans...not really just as bad or worse than these despised savages? Is not every page of our history filled with horrid deeds of treachery and murder?"

Obviously, as Ida moved freely past border after border, satisfying her long pent-up curiosity about the world, her cultural perspective, of necessity, had to broaden. But Sumatra, the island whose first European visitor, 600 years earlier, had been Marco Polo, would present an even greater challenge to her acquired equanimity.

There, she entreated Battaker tribesmen to dramatize for her their cannibal practices. After they'd overcome their reluctance to reveal this highly specific ceremonial dance, Ida found that she had to live with the consequences. "Play as it was, though, I could not witness it without some shuddering, especially when I considered that I was entirely in the power of these wild cannibals."

Moreover, the elaborate pantomime she'd just witnessed was to be the plain reality she would face only days later. Confronted in the jungle by a phalanx of spear-carrying men barring the path to her and threatening gustatory menace, Ida claims in, *A Lady's Second Journey Round the World* never to have lost her presence of mind. Hoping to seem more like a friend and less like lunch, she'd actually memorized "a little speech" in their language for just such a nasty moment. "Why, you don't mean to say you would kill and eat a woman, especially such an old one as I am! I must be very hard and tough!"

DESPITE HAVING SURVIVED HEADHUNTERS and cannibals, during Ida's final voyage saw her falling victim to a capricious ruler whose idea of hospitality took the form of shutting her in prison. Ranavalona, the insecure and paranoid queen of Madagascar, believed Pfeiffer to be part of a larger plot to overthrow her. During one angry rampage, she imperiously jailed courtiers, European visitors, and townsmen, while feeding more unfortunates to the crocodiles. Yet, after this flurry of violence, Queen Ranavalona ordered guards to release the Europeans and escort them to the coast. Unfortunately, this grueling journey lasted 50 days, during which Ida contracted a debilitating tropical fever. Though she managed to return to Vienna, she died there in 1858.

I have "no fear of death," Ida Pfeiffer had long ago written. Her courage throughout her life proved this to be true. ■

"In an age which is cynical

about the forces that push mankind,

the wild country fills

[my husband and me] with

wonderment and with enthusiasm."

YVA MOMATIUK
1940 -

PHOTOJOURNALIST YVA MOMATIUK is a professional nomad. Along with her husband John Eastcott, she has for nearly a quarter of a century been making herself at home in some of the world's more isolated regions.

Yet whether she's describing the tolerant child-rearing practices of a remote Inuit settlement north of the Arctic Circle or the chorus of sounds unleashed by nightfall in a teeming Louisiana swamp, her philosophy of travel continually breaks through. These thoughts, distilled over thousands of miles, help to give a sense of the very special universe she inhabits—the one she carries along with her wherever she happens to be.

For Momatiuk, seeking harmony with each new environment—"We live where we are in that moment, in that very place"—is less a goal than an innate way of being. And her ease at adapting to new and often difficult situations is as much about her passion to do so as it is the result of hard-won skills.

Born in Warsaw in 1940, Yva experienced a childhood marked by the inescapable realities of Europe during and after the Second World War. Her native Poland was nothing more or less than a country devastated, "squirming under a forcibly installed Communist regime…besieged by shortages of everything, from money and prospects to housing and food."

Yet, wisely, her parents—her father was an engineer, her mother a lawyer—understood that, amid such political and economic uncertainty, a young girl would benefit from a "solid" foundation to hold on to. In Yva's case, this meant that each summer she found herself joyously released into the freedom of the countryside, away from the confines and privations of daily Warsaw life.

As a practical matter, this annual escape required a train trip south from the city lasting 13 hours. But, each time, just as her excited anticipation became unbearable, the train would deposit her, finally, at a station in the foothills of the Tatra Mountains, near Poland's border with Czechoslovakia. Wandering through this Carpathian landscape, she found herself mesmerized both by the near-sinister beauty of the region and by the fierce pride of its people.

There, at the age of eight, Yva enthusiastically used a camera for the first time, deciding to try out her skills with an artistic shot that featured an immense boulder by a mountain stream. However, presented with the resulting black-and-white print, she amusedly recalls that she was fascinated by the way the many shades of green in her careful composition now were represented by a variety of grays! Yva continued to hike, snap photos, and learn back-country skills throughout her adolescent years.

In 1965, Yva, whose degrees were in architecture and urban planning, entered an international design competition. Her team of three was awarded the second prize out of a field of 900 contenders. Because East-West relationships were starting to improve, the U.S. State Department invited Yva and her co-winners to visit Polish-speaking architects in the United States. After participating in the coveted cultural-exchange, she soon found herself in New York City, where she received an offer to stay on in a permanent job at an elite architectural firm.

Yet, despite this earned—and enviable—place "at the center of things," Momatiuk, eight years later, recognized in her heart that she was ready to leave behind not just the skyscrapers of New York but the security that working on them had offered her. Craving that sense of splendid wildness she'd so relished during those long-ago childhood months of freedom, she chose willingly to forsake a settled career and, more particularly, "that certain thing looming ahead as the predestined future."

Hired as a ranch hand in Wyoming (her pay was $60 a week with room and board), Yva was a veteran of three years of working round-ups when one day, on a whim, she opted to take the longer, scenic route back from picking up a load of grain in Jackson. Spotting a hitchhiker whose own truck had broken down, she took pity on him.

John Eastcott had embarked upon his journey to that fateful encounter on that dusty back road in the American west starting from a place even farther away and more exotic than Yva—New Zealand. And he, too, had corrected course mid-stream, switching from an academic career in mathematics to freelance photography.

"We had both left our countries to study and to work," Yva says, "but we had felt a growing conviction that, had we continued our city-bound lives, the proverbial four walls of apartments, schools and offices would surely kill in us what we cherished most: the sense of discovery.

"Running into each other near the Grand Tetons and discovering how much we already shared was just a formality—yet it was also a stroke of luck. We were poor and had no idea what to do next, but we discovered we had complementary skills."

Pooling their talent was the obvious solution. But once they had begun living and working together, sharing an equal byline, it took the daily rigors of their first NATIONAL GEOGRAPHIC assignment, as they spent five months in the Canadian Arctic in 1976, to trigger the next step: matrimony. Yva describes the time as, "incredibly romantic alone together, battling adversity, surrounded by beauty." If they could get along in such difficult circumstances—at one point, stranded by weather at a distant tiny outpost, they actually teetered on the brink of starvation—they reasoned that they could surely survive the difficulties of marriage.

And, so, John proposed.

However, there were other benefits besides their "engagement" resulting from the growling stomachs they experienced at storm-locked Hope Bay. Unable any longer to ignore, or lie about, the discomforts of their hunger, they offered to share their supplies as well as partake in the scant rations of the nearest Inuit family.

For Yva and John, attuned to the subtleties of the insular society in which they'd immersed themselves, the true significance of their new friends' generosity went much deeper than the seemingly casual invitation to eat fish together. Though the offer had been extended seemingly on the spur of the moment, the grateful beneficiaries understood that, in that land of constant limits, such hospitality could never be extended carelessly.

"No longer were we passing birds with no ties," Yva would later write. The decision to feed them had, in fact, been an act of adoption.

THE AIR HAD BEEN COLD ON THE May evening when they'd flown in to the settlement of Umingmaktok. (This Inuit name translates as "where the musk oxen are many," harking back to a past era when herds were plentiful across the tundra.) The single-engine plane, after crossing the empty spaces of the Northwest Territories had adroitly managed to set them down on a mere nine feet of sea ice.

Suddenly materializing on snowmobiles, two Inuit families arrived to greet them, unable to hide their amusement at the "nylon daintiness" of the tents they helped Yva and John set up. Eventually the newcomers, after a day spent putting their gear in order, went out to meet at least a few of their cautiously watchful neighbors. It had been 65 years earlier that white strangers, called *qablunaat*, had first been seen in the Umingmaktok region. Ever since, according to Momatiuk, the formulaic response to such unlooked-for intrusions had reflected the innate Inuit attitude towards all events beyond their control.

"*Ajurnamat!* " they say. "It cannot be helped!"

In addition, curiosity is usually kept in check and questions form little part of the Inuit conversational repertoire. Yet when a rare interrogative moment did occur, soon after Yva and John's arrival, the response Yva gave was certainly the last one her questioner expected to hear.

"Sitting on the floor of a canvas tent at the fishing camp, I was fighting my first battle with a raw, tough-skinned trout, gnawing at it vigorously, when the young wife of Tikhak, the Umingmaktok store manager, blurted out:

"'Where do you live?'"

"Hesitation. Where did we live? On Great Slave Lake, where we had summered with Cree and Dogrib Indians the previous year? In the Utah ranch cabin where we had spent the winter? In our pickup truck, left 400 miles south as a raven flies? In my native Poland? In John's New Zealand? I pointed in the direction of our camp:

"'We live here.'"

FOR THE INUIT, LIVING FROM what the land provided, days of plenty regularly alternated with days of hunger. Rarely did they sit down to meals, preferring to snack whenever hungry. In the Arctic environs of Umingmaktok, such items as caribou tongue, seagull eggs, dried fish, and fried bread, all washed down with gallons of tea, were among the staples Yva and John sampled.

And, sometimes, even the *qablunaat* could prove their worth: During one period of diminished supplies, remembering her childhood mornings in the Polish forest, Yva invited some Inuit children to help her gather and cook wild mushrooms. It was the first time the group in camp had tasted such a delicacy, although Yva firmly explains, "We never meant to teach anything new, the way missionaries and other white people had tried to do."

In turn the Inuit had their own particular delicacy— blubber-wrapped seal flippers, buried until thoroughly rancid. Much to Yva's and John's disappointment they were discouraged from eating this treat. They were also steered away from tasting another delicacy, rotten loon, a dish they were less eager to sample.

"JOHN AND I DECIDED TO PROCEED TO Buchan Bay camp on foot. We asked Tikhak how to get there. Although he wanted to see us safe, he would not describe the way. Over and over he said, "I don't know," which meant: "How can I tell you? There are so many ways to get there. I do not know which is best for you.

"This is a common trait. If I tried to encourage someone to show me a task I knew he performed well, I was often informed that, yes, there were people who could do it, but he was certainly the last person to ask. Once, after a day of caribou hunting, John returned to camp with Hakungak and his brother, Akana. I served some food, saying, "I am sure you know that John has a worthless wife. My bannock [fried bread] falls apart, the seal is overcooked, and the tea cold. I cannot cook or sew. I do not know why John keeps me. And look at this fish: Is this any way to cut it? It is a disgrace! I am ashamed!"

John enjoyed my game, especially when I wailed, "And look at this man! Home he comes with empty hands! While other hunters bring good meat and fat seals, he plays with his cameras like a child and is of no use at all. It must be my fault that I couldn't get a better man, being as ugly as I am!

Akana smiled, leaned toward my disgraced mate, and said, "sweet girl." Both brothers looked pleased. This was the way to talk."

As with any first love, the enchantments of Umingmaktok endure even as it has been joined by a roster of other "homes" in their far-flung affections. ("Probably the thing that keeps us doing it more than anything else is a certain excitement which comes from planning the next year of your life," Yva says.)

It was there, after all, that they honed those instincts that still tell them how to slow down and listen. One could say they perfected at Umingmaktok the ability to offer their respect to other cultures by the mirror of both their behavior and their cameras.

OVER THE ALMOST QUARTER CENTURY since they first lived among the people of Umingmaktok, Yva and John have stayed in continuous touch with the friends they made there. They have returned when they could, and have continued to follow the fortunes of this fragile culture, still so tied to its past by the immutability of its topography yet now receiving e-mail and running a Web page. Their own role in documenting Umingmaktok's past is important to them.

As Momatiuk recently noted, "Photographs we took in the Arctic 22 years ago...are already archival. This kind of life doesn't exist anymore." She adds, "We caught the tail end of a changing world, and we've seen the influx of the new."

"I haven't photographed in any place which I detested and felt I never want to come back to again," admits Momatiuk. "In fact, what we've done in the past is we don't go to the capacity of the place, don't photograph everything, don't go everywhere.

"For us, the ideal arrangement consists of a tarp thrown on the ground in some remote and wild place, with our sleeping bags on top of the tarp. We walk, photograph, and watch the darkening sky sliding into night. And every morning we feel an enormous surge of joy: Here comes the light. We feel the sense of privilege of just being there. And we take this clean sense of a new beginning the way a painter takes a fresh canvas, and explore that promise."

Drawn by the "pull of the landscape" both to raw northern regions—Labrador, Newfoundland, Alaska's Pribilof Islands—and to rugged mountain territory— New Zealand's Southern Alps, the Tatras of her own youth—Momatiuk likes to refer to the "ribs of the earth" when she speaks of her preferred destinations.

"Stick me on a hill in the Arctic for a week and I'll be fulfilled."

Or, even more to the essential point, she declares, "I'll be fully alive." ■

FACE TO FACE
ANIMAL ENCOUNTERS

DIAN FOSSEY 1932 – 1985

BIRUTÉ GALDIKAS 1946 –

"I had a deep wish to see and live

with wild animals in

a world that hadn't yet been

completely changed by humans.

I guess I really wanted

to go backward in time....

The thought of being

where the animals haven't all been

driven into little corners

attracts me so much."

DIAN FOSSEY
1932 – 1985

"I SHALL NEVER FORGET my first encounter with gorillas.... Sound preceded sight and odor preceded both in the form of an overwhelming, musky, barnyard yet humanlike stench. The air was suddenly rent by a high-pitched series of screams followed by the rhythmic rondo of sharp pok-pok chest-beats from a great silverback male obscured behind what seemed an impenetrable wall of vegetation.... Peeking through the vegetation, we could distinguish an equally curious phalanx of black, leather-countenanced, furry-headed primates peering back at us. Their bright eyes darted nervously from under heavy brows as though trying to identify us as familiar friends or possible foes."

OF THE TWO SORTS OF NONHUMAN companions that helped keep the loneliness of Dian Fossey's early life at bay, only one was a warm-blooded mammal. That was the horse, her first love. A dedicated rider, she was expert enough in the saddle to spend part of one post-college summer as a hired hand working at a Montana dude ranch.

But, away from the stables, her childhood years in her own home were barren. That is, whenever she expressed to her parents her aching yearnings for animal companionship, she would encounter firm resistance. Animals were dirty, she was told, and, thus, with no other choices available to her, a solitary goldfish became her only pet.

Goldie, as the fish was known, was the pride of its mistress' life, although inevitably it expired in the bowl where it had peaceably swum for six years. Dian, later regarding this event as the first serious trauma of her life, would recall that she had wept inconsolably for a solid week. Ironically, the woman who later would be celebrated for her achievements as a fearless friend and protector of the endangered African mountain gorilla, was, as a little girl mourning her beloved pet fish, denied the solace of even a hamster to replace it.

BORN IN SAN FRANCISCO in 1932, Dian was six when her parents divorced. Her father, George Fossey, never of strong character, then eventually disappeared from her life. Within a year, her mother, Kitty, remarried, this time to a better provider—a contractor with profitable interests in the business world.

Unfortunately, as soon as Dian finished high school, her stepfather, Richard Price, seemed not only to expect her to pay a great deal of her own way but also insisted on pushing her in the direction of exactly the kind of office work she loathed. Ignoring him, she chose, instead, to steer her own course and soon was accepted into a program for preveterinary medical studies at the University of California at Davis.

By her second year, however, it was clear that she would need more than a passion for animals to manage passing grades in chemistry and physics. It was a career crossroads and, determined to continue in a healing profession, Dian's solution was to transfer schools and switch her major to occupational therapy.

In 1956, with the benefit of several months clinical experience in the California hospital system, she headed east to a new life in Kentucky, where she'd been offered a job as director of the therapy unit at a Louisville children's rehabilitation center.

There, many of the young patients with whom she worked had been brought for medical care from rural communities. Once removed from their home environment and expected to observe hospital protocol, her invalid charges often resembled "wild animals penned up with no hope of escape." She also noted, "They need a tremendous amount of care and kindness to make them feel life is worth living."

Dian commuted into the city each day from a

rundown farm cottage well past the edges of the city in the Kentucky countryside, where, to her great pleasure, both domestic and wild animals were in plentiful supply.

As she tried on the role of a popular young woman about town, attracting but inevitably rejecting admirers, Dian was still enough of a spiritual seeker to be influenced temporarily by a charming local priest. Her subsequent conversion to Catholicism, though short-lived, was an act that gave disproportionate distress to her mother back in California.

As early as the year after her move to Kentucky, a tantalizing vision of Africa ("where the animals haven't all been driven into little corners") had begun working its way steadily and deeply into her imagination. Much later, she was to tell an interviewer, "I had this great urge, this need to go to Africa. I had it the day I was born." But, in fact, it was probably hearing the vivid anecdotes of a Louisville acquaintance, a journalist just returned from Africa in 1957, that triggered intense longings to see it for herself.

When a close friend made a safari three years later— inviting Dian, who, sorrowfully, couldn't afford to join her—the result was that she began at once to scrimp, hoping to put aside enough for an African visit of her own. (She was "saving every penny," she wrote her mother, who, naturally, disapproved of this as she had of all her daughter's other enthusiasms.)

In the acknowledgements of her book, *Gorillas in the Mist* (1983), Dian graciously first offered thanks to the members of a generous Louisville family, the Henrys, whose collateral loan had helped her put together the $5,000 she'd estimated the seven-week trip to Africa would cost. She had agreed to mortgage her salary for the

BOB CAMPBELL

*During Dian Fossey's early years at Karisoke,
her research camp, she nursed two baby gorillas named
Pucker Puss and Coco back to health. The feeding
(and burping) schedule maintained, she explained, "would
do justice to the fussiest maternity ward."*

next three years at the exorbitant rate of 24 percent interest, since nothing mattered to her in the long run if, in
the short, she could finally get to Africa.

ARRIVING IN NAIROBI IN September of 1963, she was
recovering from one of her regular bouts of pneumonia,
and carrying 60 pounds of excess baggage. Some large
portion of this weight, at least, was taken up by her 44-
pound medicine chest; its contents were necessary for an
allergy sufferer like Dian, prone to asthma attacks and
assorted respiratory ailments.

Accompanied by a "Great White" guide whom, to
her disappointment, she found quite unsympathetic, she
began to make her way through Kenya and Tanganyika
(now Tanzania) and on into the Congo (now Zaire.) She
had already fulfilled one crucial aspect of her dream journey when, a week into her stay, she'd taken the chance
of finding legendary anthropologist Dr. Louis Leakey at
his home base camp at Olduvai Gorge near the edge of
Serengeti National Park.

Though she'd fallen and wrenched her ankle there,
forcing her to rely on a walking stick, she'd delighted in
being taken seriously by Leakey, despite her status as
mere fan and amateur naturalist. She'd listened closely as
he stressed the desirability of further in-depth fieldwork
on the great apes. She also took note of his praise of the
long-term chimpanzee project, now in its third year that
was headed by his protégé. Jane Goodall in Tanganyika.
But, most gratifying of all, the charismatic Leakey had
shared her fascination with the gorillas in the Virunga
Mountains, where next she was headed.

Her intention, lame foot or no, was to attain the

hard-to-reach environs of their natural habitat, which lay above 10,000 feet en route to the summit of Mount Mikeno. This volcanic region, long the center of contentious boundary disputes, had provided the locale for a seminal study of the mountain gorillas by the American zoologist George B. Schaller. He had put in a total of 458 observation hours on the high ground of Mount Mikeno's Kabara meadow area some three years before.

DIAN FOSSEY'S VERY FIRST NEAR-GORILLA encounter was with one whose shrill screams she'd only heard while climbing on the trail. The animal had charged her lead native guide but disappeared by the time she, with her painful ankle, could catch up. Despite this injury, she summited Mikeno, later saying, "The terrain was unbelievable, almost straight up, and we had to hang on to vines to get along or go on hands and knees."

Swept away by "the physical magnificence" of the noisy group of gorillas she'd finally encountered on her next-to-last day in the mountains, she felt herself haunted by a sense of relatedness to those creatures whose distinctive part-feral, part-human smell had heralded their extraordinary presence.

It was difficult to tear herself away from her African adventure and return to daily life in Kentucky. However, she instinctively recognized that the bond that had been forged there was real and that, somehow, her destiny was linked to these "enormous, half-seen" animals.

Against all odds, this 31-year-old pediatric therapist, who'd taken leave from her job and gone recklessly into debt to finance her trip, never doubted that one day she would "return to learn more about the Virunga gorillas."

Echoing in her mind, too, were the Swahili words she'd heard the African camp cook utter when he, along with her, had caught his first sight of a gorilla at close range. *"Kweli nudugu yanga!"* he'd exclaimed.

"Surely, God, these are my kin."

"VAGUELY REMEMBERING ME as the clumsy tourist of three years earlier, Dr. Leakey's attention was drawn to some photographs and articles I had published about gorillas since my return from Africa. After a brief interview, he suggested that I become the 'gorilla girl' he had been seeking to conduct a long-term field study. Our conversation ended with his assertion that it was mandatory I should have my appendix removed before venturing into the remote wilderness of the gorillas' high altitude habitat in central Africa.

"I would have agreed to almost anything at that point and promptly made plans for an appendectomy."

As it turned out, somewhat to Dian's surprise after leaving her appendix behind in an operating room, her new mentor had merely been testing her determination in his own peculiar fashion. He hadn't actually expected her to go through with the prophylactic surgical procedure.

Leaky's interview with Fossey took place in 1966. They met during Leakey's stop in Louisville while on a lecture tour. As she waited for his decision, and for the outcome of his efforts to raise the money to cover her field expense, (she was still paying off the money she owed for her previous trip), she taught herself Swahili. Then, at the very end of that year, she received the good news that Leighton Wilkie, the backer of Jane Goodall's work, would fund her efforts as well. She was on her way back to Nairobi at last.

From there she intended to drive herself the 700 miles to the Congo, knowing that her major task would be to secure the proper paperwork from the Congolese bureaucracy that would allow her to settle in and organize her base operations.

Two years later, in 1968, the National Geographic Society's Committee for Research and Exploration also joined in supporting her. Her first report, "Making Friends with Mountain Gorillas," appeared in NATIONAL GEOGRAPHIC in January 1970, introducing Louis Leakey's supremely dedicated "gorilla girl" to the world.

"For the past three years I have spent most of my days with wild mountain gorillas. Their home, and mine, has been the misty wooded slopes of the Virunga range, eight lofty volcanoes—the highest is 14,787 feet—shared by three African nations, Rwanda, Uganda, and the Democratic Republic of the Congo.

"During this time I have become well acquainted with many of the gorillas, and they with me.... I know the gorillas as individuals, each with his own traits and personality, and mainly, for identification in my hundreds of pages of notes, I have given many of them names: Rafiki, Uncle Bert, Icarus, and so on...," Fossey wrote, making it clear that proximity had evolved into intimacy, just as she had hoped.

By learning to behave as her subjects did—which meant imitating their stylized vocalizations and body movements—she had gained their trust and even found herself accepted "almost as a member" by several of the groups she was observing.

"The textbook instructions for such studies are

merely to sit and observe," she wrote. But, preferring a different approach, she practiced the arts of hooting, grunting, and belching loudly. She made herself chew the same foliage they did, kept low to the ground when moving, and became adept at grooming herself in the gorilla manner.

"I scratched my scalp noisily.... Almost immediately [a gorilla] began to scratch. It was not clear who was aping whom," she joked. But her efforts at mimicry paid off when Peanuts, a particularly playful gorilla, overcame shyness and reached out to touch Dian's hand— possibly the first encounter ever between a wild gorilla and a human.

THE LARGEST OF THE GREAT APES, a mature male gorilla can be as tall as 6 feet and weigh 400 pounds or more, making it easy to see why one might be intimidated by an unexpected encounter. Yet, as Fossey pointed out in that earliest published article, three decades ago, the size of the mountain gorilla, *Gorilla gorilla beringe,* she was studying was no longer a guarantee against their many enemies, both natural and unnatural. Even then, her subjects were losing numbers and territory at too rapid a rate,she predicted, to guarantee their survival into the indefinite future.

Six months after Dian Fossey had established her camp at the isolated Kabara meadow site favored by George Schaller, she was rudely hauled off Mount Mikeno by armed soldiers. They explained to her that for her own well-being she would be held in a detention center.

The Belgian Congo had become the newborn political entity of Zaire, and it quickly became obvious to her that she would be safer anywhere but where she was being detained. Making her escape through a combination of bribes and stealth across the border to Uganda, she soon learned that orders had been issued to shoot her on sight were she to return to Zaire.

After a strategy meeting with Louis Leakey in Nairobi, it was decided that she would return to the Virungas—but to the Rwandan side of the mountains. She was not at all tempted by his suggestion that, owing to the unpredictable political climate, she might forsake her mountain gorillas for the lowland ones of West Africa, or for the orangutans of Asia.

She also was made aware of the rather shocking news that she had already been declared "missing and presumed dead" by the U.S. State Department. Yet, her overriding thought was only that "there were still gorillas to find and mountains to climb," and within two weeks she was reestablishing contact, miraculously, with some of the same wandering gorilla groups she had known at Kabara.

They "recognized me and held their ground at about 50 feet. I was able to see that an infant had been born since I left." This unexpected contact with familiar gorilla faces, she wrote, was "one of the most wonderful welcome-home gifts" she could ever imagine.

NOTHING ABOUT THE LIFE DIAN FOSSEY chose to lead in Africa over the course of the next 18 years could be said to be easy. Like the endangered animals that were her beloved obsession, she was continually driven to protect herself from the hostile onslaughts of nature as well as from the more intentional villainies of human agents.

One catalogue of a day's possible obstacles in the volcanic highlands included: climbing up 45-degree slopes, wading through mud, hacking through towers of vegetation, and crawling through stinging foliage. "Most people," she wrote, "when thinking of Africa, envision dry plains sweltering under a never-ending sun. When I think of Africa I think only of the montane rain forest of the Virungas—cold and misty, with an average annual rainfall of 72 inches."

But it was the unnatural enemies who were to be her undoing in the end—and an extremely ghastly end it was. The only possible consolation one could take is that she met it in the one place on the planet she most wanted to be and had claimed as her very own.

A CELEBRITY REVERED IN THE WORLD that lay beyond the mountains, Dian remained a fierce and immovable threat to the poachers, herdsmen, hunters, black marketers and other exploiter-despoilers whose plans and desires ran counter to her own. They placed in constant peril everything for which she had worked for so long.

In the months before her life ended, she'd been troubled by "a general sense of unease about the gorillas," as well as erratic patterns of behavior among them she had never seen before and couldn't explain. Nor, closer to home, could she feel comfortable with the near-fatal poisoning of her two parrots or the many other threats she received as she picked up her efforts. But despite the increasing risk, she continued her battle, once saying, "If I can enforce the rules of a supposedly protected park against the slaughter of animals, then I must do it."

Her research camp, Karisoke—named after two of the Virunga mountains, Karisimbi and Visoke—had officially been set up on September 24, 1967. Her body would be found there, inside her house, on December 27, 1985, her skull split by an unknown assailant.

Called by the natives *Nyiramachabelli*—the old lady who lives in the forest without a man—she beautifully explained herself and her life in *Gorillas in the Mist*. "As a pioneer I sometimes did endure loneliness," she wrote, "but I have reaped a tremendous satisfaction that followers will never be able to know." ■

"The apes' mouths were like bottomless pits. I once took two flashlight batteries out of Sugito's mouth. Satisfied he was 'clean,' I was just going to leave when he rolled out another on onto his bottom lip.... Sobiarso would eat flashlight bulbs and both she and Rio would suck all the fountain pens dry. It was a battle of wits, and they won!"

BIRUTÉ GALDIKAS
1946 –

S HE CONSIDERED THEM as her own children and because she was living far from home, Biruté Galdikas made many allowances for their unmannerly behavior. Whether they were greedy or stubborn, threw violent tantrums, bit each other, or simply screamed at the top of their lungs, her response was to stay tolerant. And when, being strong for their ages, they would exhibit destructive tendencies (shredding pillows and mattresses, poking holes in the walls), she went about straightening up the mess, hoping they'd eventually grow out of these bad habits.

How then, could she ever imagine that the first-born of this energetic brood, a particularly bright seven-year-old, would one day go far, far beyond the kind of ordinary mischief he was already known for? Far enough, in fact, apparently to kill, unrepentantly, one of his playmates in cold blood?

It was the ultimate maternal nightmare.

For primatologist Galdikas, the fact that Sugito wasn't the sort of underage murderer-next-door who tops the nightly news, but rather a young orangutan she'd adopted, made the situation she found herself in more painful. Her intention had been to rehabilitate him back into his natural habitat, but she was encountering difficulties she had never envisioned.

She was, after all, well aware, after years spent living in Indonesian Borneo in intimate proximity to these great red apes, that "wild adult orangutans are predominantly solitary and usually very nonaggressive, gentle creatures. They have never been observed to kill."

Thus, what she quickly realized—her distress made greater by this unsuspecting complicity—was her own role in the tragedy, despite her best efforts to raise him as an orangutan:

"I faced the dreadful consequences of inadvertently raising an orangutan as a human being."

BORN TO LITHUANIAN PARENTS WHO emigrated to Canada in 1948, Biruté Galdikas traces her lifelong fascination with the natural sciences to the collections of wriggling tadpoles and salamanders she scooped up in a

Toronto park not far from her house. Yet, in her early desire to penetrate the secrets of the world around her, she didn't concentrate only on what she could touch or pick up. Her horizons were already larger: "There were mature oaks in our backyard, and I used to lie under them, look up at the stars and...wonder."

Certainly, when contemplating the vastness of the universe and its unfathomable distance from oneself, there are more questions than answers. But a child is a perpetual curiosity machine, and the deliciousness of the sensation of not-knowing/longing-to-know lies at the heart of Galdikas's childhood memories of her contemplative moments. In fact, such a precocious affinity for wondering has lasted a lifetime for Biruté and has engendered a career.

It was above all the idea of prehistory, humankind's beginnings, that took hold of her imagination and lured her on. And she had long known—graduate school in anthropology only serving to confirm her instinct about what she was meant to do—that she wanted to focus exclusively, and from as up close as possible, on *Pongo pygmaeus*, the only Asian great ape: the orangutan.

Her reasons for fixing on orangutans, she says, were simple. She has often described how she kept being haunted by the way their eyes "mirrored our own." (Orangutans, especially the younger ones, not only have human-seeming faces, but, unlike gorillas and chimpanzees, they resemble us in having white visible around the iris.) The word orangutan actually translates from the Malay as "person of the forest."

But the other explanation for her choice springs from a deeper, more personal vein of inquiry, one as rooted in the intellectual fiber of Biruté Galdikas as those massive oak trees of her childhood. She still wanted to know "where we came from." And for her, she says, "it was not just a scientific but a spiritual quest."

IN 1969, WHILE A GRADUATE student at UCLA, Biruté attended a lecture by Dr. Louis Leakey, the archaeologist and anthropologist whose headline-making fossil finds in East Africa a decade earlier had moved back the birth date for *Homo sapiens*. She knew already that Leakey believed that careful, steady observation of the world's great apes over time would reveal surprising truths about their links to those human ancestors whose bones he had unearthed. With this result in mind, he'd functioned as an important mentor to two women already gaining attention for their fieldwork with primates, Jane Goodall and Dian Fossey.

Biruté took her seat in the audience, somehow convinced that if she could get him to listen to her, her future would be changed. Yet it wasn't until she heard him actually mention his ties to Goodall's chimpanzee project that a sense of inevitability came over her. Her orangutans—the ones she'd never yet seen in the wild but yearned to reach—became, suddenly, that much more real to her.

Dr. Leakey, for his part, did listen when she approached him after his talk and was impressed by her passion and determination. He also approved of the habits of sharp awareness she displayed when he set her a series of odd little tests. Having satisfied himself that she possessed the right stuff—the necessary courage, brains, and staying power—to take on such a challenge, he agreed to back her effort (as did the National Geographic Society).

It was an instant credibility boost: Biruté Galdikas, at 25, had arrived suddenly on the world stage of anointed animal people, an elite group privileged to be able to follow their obsessions to some of the Earth's more remote corners. And $9,000, the amount Leakey managed to raise on her behalf in two and a half years, was for 1971 a not inconsiderable sum. Surely it would go far in the rain forests of Indonesia.

"Travel was so different 30 years ago," Galdikas points out, nostalgic now for the sense of romance that accompanied the once arduous, time-consuming trip.

"Today you have direct flights to Asia. But back then it was an endless journey, changing in Honolulu and in Guam, where planes left only three time a week. By the time we got to Borneo it had an almost dreamlike quality."

OF COURSE, SHE COULDN'T HAVE KNOWN as she flew over the Pacific with only a backpack and three NATIONAL GEOGRAPHICs, that Tanjung Puting Reserve, the 14-square-mile study area to which she was heading, would be the center of her life for the next three decades. What she did know, however, was that even the U.S. government maps she carried with her left something to be desired in the way of providing specific information. For example, they unhelpfully revealed "altitude unknown," when she checked her destination.

Borneo is the world's third-largest island, with more than 70 percent of its territory occupied by Indonesian Borneo (or Kalimantan, as it is known to Indonesians). Yet despite its size, it is sparsely populated and, as the deficient map indicated, never has been well explored or accurately charted, owing to vast areas of inhospitable terrain.

Nor should one suppose that the thick jungle, mangrove swamps, and weed-clogged rivers are all that count as unwelcoming in the matter of Borneo's interior. As Galdikas has written in her memoir, *Reflections of Eden: My Years with the Orangutans of Borneo* (1995), "The true hazards of the rain forest were little nagging things like viruses, parasites, insects, and plant toxins. The leeches were so abundant that we lost track of how many we took off our bodies in the course of any one day."

ARRIVING WITH HER HUSBAND, photographer Rod Brindamour, (to whom she would stay married for more than 13 years), what Galdikas found was in every way "totally wilderness." Daunting, stimulating, and ghastly all at the same time, it did cause her despair in her earliest weeks. Yet, mesmerized by her glimpses of the elusive creatures she had come to understand and learn from, she managed to keep going, ignoring as best she could the leeches and other discomforts.

"There were no guides or guidebooks [to explain] who all the animals were. It took me a year to get it all straight. I saw common monkeys and had to figure out what they were. Wild pigs, Malay bears, elephants, crocodiles, and king cobras are included in the native fauna, while rhinoceroses, once numerous, have been hunted nearly to extinction.

"And I didn't even know whether we would encounter headhunters," she admits. After all, travelers' reports from Borneo in the 19th century, including those of Ida Pfeiffer, had made the island celebrated for its headhunters, and, according to Biruté, as late as the 1960s there had still been outbreaks.

Previous researchers attempting to study the orangutans of Borneo (their only other native habitat is found on northern Sumatra) had never made much headway, discouraged by the adverse conditions. Galdikas, reading their work in order to familiarize herself with what to expect, was struck by how many seemed to be accounts of sodden hour after sodden hour spent keeping watch.

"I honestly believed I'd be spending all my time in swamps up to my neck." And when the first orangutans she saw, a mother and her daughter, indeed were spotted inaccessibly at the edge of one, "I kept believing this."

"In social behavior the orangutan has always been considered very different not only from humans, but also from other monkeys and apes, including its African cousins, the gorilla and chimpanzee. Primates have been characterized as social animals par excellence, but the wild orangutans Rod and I saw in those early months were almost invariably solitary: lone males or adult females accompanied by their dependent young."

Yet, says Galdikas, "I knew that orangutans must meet and interact—if only to breed—and I longed to know the full extent of such relationships."

Her initial encounter with one of her subjects at ground level (instead of in the forest canopy the animals prefer) came as she was limping back to camp in the rain. "My left leg was soaked with blood from a wound made by my machete, which had slipped as I cut a vine." At the time she could hardly believe what she was seeing: an orangutan silently crossing through the tall grass of a field. However, it wasn't long before she had logged enough sightings to know this wasn't as rare an occurrence as previously believed.

Galdikas even confirmed that orangutans, who ordinarily build new sleeping nests for themselves every night high in the trees, may sometimes break that pattern. "I was amazed to see a subadult male sleep for 45 minutes on the ground during the day. He didn't make a nest but merely bent a sapling under him as he lay down."

One vivid recollection is of the blistering hot day she came face-to-face with another large adult male traveling on the ground. "It was almost a showdown. I was rounding a turn...when a huge orangutan appeared, heading straight toward me. He was just ambling along head down, oblivious to my presence. Then he stopped dead in his tracks less than 12 feet away. For long seconds he stared and stared. I guess he was evaluating the bizarre sight of a pale-faced primatologist with large black sunglasses, clutching an enormous bag of dirty laundry."

THROUGHOUT BIRUTÉ'S 30 YEARS at Tanjung Puting Reserve, however, some of the greatest moments of drama, humor, and heartbreak have been associated with the rehabilitant orangutans. These are weaned, usually with great difficulty, from a variety of civilization's bad habits and returned to the wild. Whether kidnapped by poachers, left homeless by land clearing or logging, retired

In her role as a surrogate mother trying to accustom her young charges to their natural habitat, Biruté Galdikas gains firsthand experience of the way baby orangutans can cling to their mothers.

from zoos, or discarded by laboratories, these orangutans usually have been given every reason to be dysfunctional.

Sugito, the first such foundling to be taken in, was one year old when he arrived at Camp Leakey (named in tribute to her patron) and had no trouble whatsoever accepting Biruté as his mother. But since orangutan infants cling to their mom until they're four and are not totally weaned until seven, "even shifting him from one part of my body to another involved much fighting and howling."

Sugito also greedily tasted anything that came his way, from a bottle of antiseptic to flashlight batteries, and he enjoyed spitting his mouthfuls of chewed food into Biruté's tea. With his fellow "orange monster-babies" he vied to sneak into bed with Biruté and Rod in the middle of the night, the apes eventually crowding the two humans off their mattress.

But as he grew older, Sugito grew more and more unpredictable and what had been merely maddening now was potentially dangerous. In her role as surrogate parent, Biruté, too late, had come to recognize her limitations: "I lacked the orangutan mother's powerful jaws and large canines that enforce a juvenile's quick and painless independence."

Now, unfortunately, Sugito had grown up to become the ape equivalent of a charming serial killer, with an m.o. that involved attempting to drown very young female victims of whom he was jealous by holding them face down in the river.

No legal system existed at Tanjung Puting ready to step in and adjudicate; there were no prosecutors and no defenders—only sadness. In the end, relates Galdikas, even though Sugito did eventually stop killing, it was clear that he would have to be banished from the only home he'd known since he had been rescued from imprisonment in a small crate six years earlier.

After he'd made a particularly destructive raid on the Galdikas house, Biruté finally accepted the heart-breaking fact that her first child of the forest would have to be released far from the camp, and forced to survive on his own. Biruté never knew for certain if she would ever see the orphaned orangutan again. Yet, years later, after several male orangutans who clearly knew her visited the camp, Biruté began to believe in the possibility that one was a mature and now very different-looking Sugito.

WITH ROD BRINDAMOUR, BIRUTÉ GALDIKAS had one son, Binti Paul. With her second husband, Pak Bohap bin Jalan, a Dayak tribal president whom she married in 1981 and who is codirector of her orangutan project, she has a son and a daughter, Frederick and Filomena Jane.

In 1998, the combination of Indonesian drought and burned forests forced Biruté to supplement the apes' diet with daily drop-offs of fruit. "I'm still continuing the research," Galdikas explains, "I depend on trained Dayak assistants and Indonesian students. But the most pressing issue is the coming disappearance of orangutans in the wild as poaching and loss of habitat have made them endangered."

Her years of laboring devotedly, of thinking, writing, and studying about her great apes, make her vantage point a powerful one. And her passion has never abated: "I feel the world is indifferent to the destruction of their habitat. We share this fragile home planet with many other creatures, and it is up to us to respect and protect them." ■

GLOBE-TROTTERS

ISABELLA BIRD BISHOP
1831 – 1904

DERVLA MURPHY
1931 –

"The elephant...was brought below the porch. They are truly hideous beasts, with their gray, wrinkled, hairless hides, the huge ragged 'flappers' which cover their ears...the small mean eyes, the hideous proboscis which coils itself snakishly round everything...."

ISABELLA BIRD BISHOP
1831 – 1904

"TRAVELERS ARE privileged to do the most improper things with perfect propriety, that is one charm of travelling."

By having said that, Isabella Bird Bishop, the famed Victorian globe-trotter, creates the impression that she herself was inclined to startle or scandalize—though, in fact, wherever she turned up, this clergyman's daughter was much more likely to lead an impromptu Bible discussion or lecture on the evils of slavery than intentionally commit any social indiscretion—even when abroad.

What was decidedly improper, though—at least, as her contemporaries would have defined it—was Isabella's never-sated addiction to solitary wanderings in exotic places. That is, as a middle-aged, gently reared English-woman, often wearing her own odd version of native garb, her very presence had the potential to shock—for example, when she galloped through Berber strongholds in northern Africa on a black horse with a crimson saddle or proceeded through rural China carried in an open sedan chair.

Only six years old when the young Queen Victoria embarked on her 63-year reign in 1837, and living to survive that doughty monarch by three years, Isabella certainly seems a perfect exemplar of the era she so completely inhabited. Combining pious conventionality with self-indulging eccentricity, she represents a paradigm of Victorianism in all its peculiar glory.

Isabella Bird Bishop was called by some the most prolific of the colorful sisterhood of 19th-century women explorers, who barely ever stopped to rest as they churned out book after book, article after article. She has also been labeled the most ubiquitous. "She went just about everywhere sooner or later" is how one commentator admiringly summed up the continents she crossed and recrossed. More telling still, Isabella Bird Bishop, in the more than a century and a half since her birth, frequently has been singled out as the "best-loved" of the Victorian travelers.

Nonetheless, the last word should probably go to Dr. John Bishop, the faithful Scottish physician who became her husband. (Despite repeated rejections, he'd continued to press his suit until, finally, at the age of 50, and between trips, she agreed to marry him.) Dr. Bishop, to his credit, understood his bride well enough to quip fondly: "I have only one rival in Isabella's heart, and that is the high tableland of Central Asia."

BORN IN 1831 IN THE NORTH OF England and educated at home, Isabella Lucy Bird had one younger sister, Henrietta (known as "Hennie"), to whom she was devoted. By the time they were adolescents, their father, the Reverend Edward Bird, had been attached to small village churches in Yorkshire and Cheshire, as well as given the pulpit of a large urban congregation in the industrial city of Birmingham.

During those earliest years, the precocious Isabella was spoiled by relatives and servants, even to the point of being a bit of an enfant terrible, liable to surprise adults with her pert sarcasms. A passionate reader, she would disappear into the stables with a book and soon be lost to the household until each new hiding place was known. Later a superb and even indomitable horsewoman, she learned to ride initially perched on a cushion atop her father's horse. Soon she was given a mount of her own and would proudly keep her parent company while he made his parish rounds through the rough country lanes.

After she became a celebrated traveler and writer, she would explain her vaunted powers of observation by fondly recalling those long-ago outings when it fell to her to reply accurately to her father's "conversational questioning upon everything." As they rode along together, the Reverend Mr. Bird would test her by asking about "the crops in such-and-such fields..." or "how each gate we passed through was hung, about animals seen and parishioners met."

At 18 and living with her family in central England's Wyton, in Huntingdonshire (another tiny rural parish for her father), Isabella underwent surgery for a spinal tumor. Since childhood, she had been prone to a variety of physical ailments, including insomnia and painful abscesses of the foot. She would suffer with back pain, or "spinal prostration," as it was diagnosed, for the rest of her life. Thus, because of poor health, a large part of Isabella's early twenties was passed in what her friend and one of her first biographers, Anna Stoddart, politely termed "a semi-recumbent position."

Yet despite that fact, she was already one truly astonishing adventure beyond what other sheltered young ladies, even ones far less disposed to chronic invalidism, could possibly claim. For, in 1852, at the age of 22, just after arriving in London to visit an aunt, Isabella had managed, as she left the railway station, the feat of singlehandedly thwarting an assassination attempt against a Cabinet member.

A real-life episode the equal of any of the lurid, penny-dreadful fiction of the day, the experience began when she hailed a cab and discovered on the seat a packet of documents left behind by the previous passenger. Once she'd examined the contents, hoping for clues to the owner, it quickly became clear to Isabella that what she had found were the details of a murderous political plot. Resourcefully, she was inspired to make a fast switch: Replacing the compromising papers with a set of similarly sized advertisements, she handed these to the man who appeared an instant later at the cab window seeking to reclaim his property.

Before he could protest the substitution, she commanded the driver to make all haste to the Home

Office, where she personally delivered the incriminating evidence to the minister. For the rest of that stay in London, Isabella remained under official government protection, a detective guarding her, to prevent the villains she'd so coolly circumvented from succeeding at some unpleasant revenge.

Still, nothing, not even the Bird household's annual summer stays in the bracing Scottish Highlands, seemed to have any lasting salutary effect on Isabella's vitality. She remained listless, depressed, unable to sleep. Finally, it fell to the family doctor to propose, having no other potions or pills to try, the more extreme measure of a long journey by sea as a potential restorative.

The Birds, anxious for their daughter's well-being, agreed to the trip, and so, one June morning in 1854, with their blessing and £100 spending money (her father tolerantly gave her permission to stay away as long as her funds lasted), she boarded a Cunard liner for North America. She was not completely on her own though, as she would later prefer to be when she ventured around the globe: On this maiden voyage she was respectably chaperoned by visiting Canadian cousins returning home.

Whatever she or her parents might actually have expected to result from the ocean air and change of scenery, the truth is, the prescribing physician was obviously a psychologist ahead of his time. Once under way, with Halifax, Nova Scotia, the first port of call, Isabella began to thrive. It would not be long before she would have the opportunity to put this remedy back into practice. But it almost always turned out that the best tonic for whatever ailed Isabella—including, eventually, mourning the loss of those dearest to her, whether parents, sister, husband—was to be the very act of traveling.

"It is rather a sad fact," she herself later concluded, somewhat ironically, "but rough knocking about, open-air life, in combination with sufficient interest, is the one in which my health and spirits are the best."

DURING ISABELLA'S INITIAL EXPEDITION—which lasted seven months and saw her return to England with £10 still unspent—she filled her diaries and letters home with vivid New World impressions. From the banks of the Mississippi to New York, she happily coped with an array of misfortunes, including a pickpocket and the aftermath of a cholera epidemic. She also enjoyed a lively social whirl in every city where she stopped—Cincinnati, Chicago, Detroit, Toronto, Montreal, and Boston, among them.

Upon her return home to Wyton, Isabella's father encouraged his daughter to turn her account of her trip into a narrative fit for publication. Writing easily and in a natural style, enjoying the project as much for its own sake as for the chance to reach an audience beyond family and friends, Isabella completed a manuscript draft in five months. By the summer of 1855, almost a year to the day after her departure, she was ready to take advantage of an acquaintance's referral to John Murray, the distinguished London publisher.

Though rejecting the unalluring title she'd assigned it, *The Car and the Steamboat*, Murray stood enthusiastically prepared to shepherd Miss Bird through the trials and rewards of authordom. Thus was launched a combined business relationship and personal friendship that would endure with mutual benefit and respect for nearly 40 years.

Isabella's first book, renamed *The Englishwoman in America,* was released in January of 1856, to admiring reviews and encouraging sales on both sides of the Atlantic. She found herself delighted to put to philanthropic use her not-inconsiderable profits, helping impoverished fishermen in her beloved West Highlands to purchase a fleet of much needed, deep-sea vessels.

A year later, again on medical advice, Isabella set off a second time for America, staying nearly 12 months instead of the 6 she'd intended. She revisited many of her previous haunts, but also witnessed Congress in session in Washington and braved the Canadian wilderness as far north as the Hudson Bay Territory. In New England, she spent evenings with Longfellow, Emerson, and Thoreau, and she was moved to tears in Virginia by the simple but fervent prayers she heard at an African Baptist church service.

Unfortunately, not long after she returned home, to his family's immense sorrow, Mr. Bird died. For the next 14 years, Isabella was occupied almost entirely with local good works and domestic concerns. Able to make one trip back to Canada to oversee a pet charitable project early in 1866, she faced loss again when her adored mother died that year.

In 1870, her health took such a turn for the worse that a steel contrivance was manufactured to support her head, taking pressure off her spine and confining her to bed. A voyage to New York two years after this found her too ill, upon arrival, even to take advantage of the publishing introductions she'd been given. She returned home, disappointed that the usual cure had not been effective.

By 1872, Isabella Bird, with her repeated trips to North America, already had extraordinary mileage under her petticoat. But her recent medical history and assorted personal setbacks were surely an obstacle to anyone's imagining that this spinster's major gallivanting—and subsequent worldwide renown—lay still ahead of her.

THE REGRET THAT ISABELLA, again under doctor's orders, had felt at parting from her sister Hennie was intense, especially because the two of them were suddenly alone in the world. This melancholy seized her spirits during her first weeks aboard ship, and her mood never fully lightened as she made her way through the Australian bush and New Zealand's settlements. However, after half a year spent exploring the antipodes, on the first leg of an elaborate sea journey, she set off on January 1, 1873, for what were then known as the Sandwich Islands (today the state of Hawaii), en route to San Francisco.

Her passage there, aboard a rundown old tub called the *Nevada*, was a difficult one, and yet the discomforts could exhilarate her. A furious tempest at sea, lasting 12 hours and nearly capsizing the ship, in fact, only elicited a vow of allegiance to Neptune. (Friends eventually would dub Isabella the "Stormy Petrel," because of her passion for howling winds and rain.)

"At last I am in love," she wrote, "and the old sea-god has so stolen my heart and penetrated my soul that I seriously feel that hereafter, though I must be elsewhere in body, I shall be with him in spirit! My two friends on board this ship have several times told me that I have imbibed the very spirit of the sea. It is to me like living in a new world, so free, so fresh, so vital, so careless, so unfettered, so full of interest that one grudges being asleep; and, instead of carrying cares and worries and thoughts of the morrow to bed with one to keep one awake, one falls asleep at once to wake to another day in which one knows that there can be nothing to annoy one—no door-bells, no "please mems," no dirt, no bills, no demands of any kind, no vain attempts to overtake all one knows one should do."

And the beautiful, volcano-pocked, lushly vegetated islands themselves entranced her, as she toured them avidly on horseback for seven months before taking her leave. "Farewell for ever, my bright and tropic dream!" she wrote, even having toyed momentarily with the notion of uprooting stay-at-home sister Hennie and settling with her there.

Arriving next in San Francisco, then crossing the High Sierra by train, Isabella grew obsessed by her desire to reach Estes Park, Colorado, a valley in the Rocky Mountains she'd heard was singularly breathtaking in its vistas. At last, after losing her way with the first, hapless guide she hired, she rode triumphantly into Muggins Gulch, where lay the entrance to the park. There, she hoped, in addition to the natural wonders, to catch a glimpse of its famous inhabitant, the Irish-Canadian trap-per and Indian scout "Mountain Jim" Nugent, already a legendary figure of the raw-mannered and violent West.

It was to be a momentous encounter. For, as Isabella and her companions approached his mud-roofed cabin, he appeared suddenly at the door, armed with both a revolver and a hunting knife. Her first, horrified impression was that he had 'Desperado' written in large letters all over him."

However, Jim, despite being one-eyed (he'd gotten the worst of a tussle with a grizzly bear), and clothed in what looked like rags, greeted the newcomers courteously in a cultured accent, acknowledging Isabella as a "country-woman." Softening, she grew to accept the many contradictions in his "ruffian's" nature, and as they rode, climbed, and camped together, she became his intimate confidante. Surprised at her reactions, she struggled with her attraction

Isabella Bird Bishop (at right) poses by her tent in the western

to him, only to dismiss her heightened feelings as "egregious vanity, unthinkable in a woman of forty."

The time spent sharing Jim Nugent's "breezy mountain recklessness" forms, perhaps, the most notorious episode of Isabella's career; and her thrilling book, *A Lady's Life in the Rocky Mountains* (1879), is one of her

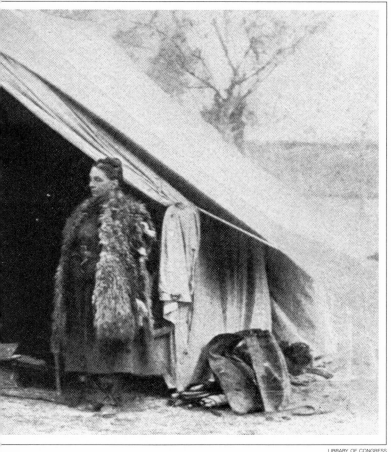

region of Persia after a grueling 46-day trek by mule from Baghdad.

best and most popular. Though Jim had been "a man any woman might love," she understood equally that he was "a man no sane woman would marry." Even before he had put her on a departing stagecoach, she had been compelled to declare, "There can be nothing between us but constraint." The following year, when Jim was shot by an enemy in an quarrel, Isabella regretfully heard the news two continents away in Switzerland.

BACK IN SCOTLAND, where she and Hennie now kept residences both in Edinburgh and on the Isle of Mull, she had a different sort of admirer to keep at bay, the eminently reliable, highly respectable Dr. John Bishop, (though to him she made the excuse of not wishing to be "an invalid wife.") Escaping to Japan—an exotic destination for anyone in 1878, let alone a solitary Englishwoman—she tramped around, wearing a tweed riding habit and a bowl-shaped bamboo hat, and, when on horseback, had nothing but contempt for her ill-favored Japanese mounts. Hong Kong, the Malayan Peninsula, and Egypt rounded out this expedition, which gave rise to two memoirs, *Unbeaten Tracks in Japan* (1880) and *The Golden Chersonese* (1883).

But on the voyage home, Isabella fell ill. As her strength returned in Edinburgh, she received a letter from Hennie asking her to come to Mull, for she was ill. At once Isabella left for the cottage that the two sisters often shared. But when she arrived, the housekeeper informed her, "I can do no more for your sister. She has typhoid fever. I have sent for Dr. Bishop."

For five weeks Isabella nursed her sister under Dr. Bishop's guidance. When Hennie died, only then did her sad survivor make a turnabout and marry Dr. Bishop, at this point ceasing to travel. It was enough for her to be a well-liked and busy physician's helpmate.

But, after treating a sailor with the skin disease erysipelas, which infected him as well, John Bishop, who was ten years younger than his wife, began to experience poor health. In 1886, even after the famed surgeon Sir Joseph Lister had attempted one of the first blood transfusions, Dr. Bishop died.

While mourning—before she headed out to Central Asia—Isabella involved herself in such activities as temperance lecturing, organizing for the YWCA, delivering soup to the sick or needy, and giving French lessons to Scottish children. The widow Bishop also took a strenuous course in nursing at a London hospital, now finding Scotland too associated with grief. Of her late husband she noted, "His long and weary illness made him the object of all my thoughts. I have lived for him.... Henceforth I must live my own life."

FOR MOST OF THE NEXT DOZEN YEARS, Isabella Bird Bishop stayed in motion. She more or less dismissed India, after crossing from Pakistan to Little Tibet (Ladakh.) She felt in greater sympathy with the Buddhist society in the more remote corners of Ladakh, reached only after a daunting 26-day journey through jagged mountain passes, than she did with the people of colonial India who seemed to her artificially "civilized."

Having learned to ride "yak back," among the Tibetan nomads, she next went on "saddle mule" for 46 frigid days from Baghdad to Tehran, fulfilling her desire to see Persia (now Iran). In the course of this nightmarish ordeal,

Isabella lost 22 pounds. The thousand-mile trip across Kurdistan with an unruly caravan that came next, even plagued by brigands and evil weather, seemed practically child's play.

Isabella published *Journeys in Persia and Kurdistan* in 1891, and the following year, she became the first woman ever invited to address the Royal Geographical Society at one of its London meetings. This honor stood as no cap to her career but rather only a resting place. In 1894, she traveled to Korea and China where, forsaking horseback, she rode in a sedan chair—made of bamboo, it was perched on top of 14-foot poles and carried by three bearers—a small nod, at last, to her advancing age and chronic back pain.

That conveyance, however, hardly answered for the entire 8,000 miles she totaled, an eighth of which was covered on the proverbial "slow boat" up the Yangtze. She had also by now become adept at the new skill of photography and shot many scenes from the deck, which can be seen in the book entitled *The Yangtze Valley and Beyond* (1900).

Isabella's final travel adventure was to North Africa in 1901. It was then that this indomitable 70 year old rode with a companion through the Atlas Mountains, laming two horses in the process and losing a pack mule over a precipice. She wrote to one correspondent, "You would fail to recognize your infirm friend astride a superb horse in full blue trousers and a short full skirt, with great brass spurs belonging to the generalissimo of the Moorish army, and riding down places where a rolling stone or a slip would mean destruction. I never expected to do such travelling again." And though she was no stranger to royalty—having been received by Queen Victoria, as well as the King and Queen of Korea—she took immodest pride in being able to pronounce herself "the only European woman who has ever seen an Emperor of Morocco!"

Arriving back in Tangier, after narrowly evading a band of armed horsemen in hot pursuit of her party outside the city limits, Isabella was prostrated from exhaustion. By the time she arrived home in England, her health was too shattered for repair—a truth especially apparent when she seemed no longer to relish her food. (According to her late husband, she had long enjoyed "the appetite of a tiger and the digestion of an ostrich.") Delicacies sent to tempt her arrived daily on her doorstep from well-wishers all over Great Britain. But now in rented rooms in Edinburgh where she was being lovingly nursed, she was steadily failing and knew it.

To friends in China, she wrote of her packed bags, sitting ready in London for the Trans-Siberian Railway trip she'd scheduled and now understood that she would be unable to take. "My heart was greatly set on this, and when I left London, I left there my luggage packed for Peking.... I got here and think it more than likely that my next journey will be to the grave of my kindred in Dean Cemetery."

ISABELLA BIRD BISHOP died nearly 11 months later. Half of a fitting epitaph might be found in these thoughts from her friend, Anna Stoddart: "Tent life always suited her, and in spite of alarms she enjoyed the absolute novelty of her experiences. Without alarms and difficulties she would probably have accounted her venture a failure."

The other half could echo her own last words, "Oh, what a shouting there will be!" ■

"I presented myself to the
Afghan Embassy...only to be told
that under no circumstance...
would they grant a visa to a woman
who intended cycling alone through
Afghanistan. Apparently, six years ago,
a lone Swedish woman was
carved up into small pieces,
since [then] solitary female travelers
have been banned....
It looks as though I'm beaten....
However, I've a few...
schemes to be tried tomorrow."

DERVLA MURPHY
1931 –

The year was 1963, and Dervla Murphy was fulfilling a long-held dream—to bicycle across Europe by herself, making India her final destination. Not yet the legendary figure she would become, she was then exactly what she seemed to be: A sturdy and determined 31-year-old Irishwoman, unknown to the world at large, proceeding doggedly through scorching deserts and over harrowing mountain paths. More than a thousand miles away from home, she was in the middle of an adventure-rich, purely personal odyssey that she'd thought about for most of her life and prepared for all on her own.

As she cycled farther and farther eastward from her starting point, Lismore, County Waterford, Ireland, the road stretching ahead demanded all of her attention. Beneath her was the stalwart Roz, short for Rozinante, the name she'd jauntily dubbed her Armstrong Cadet man's bike. Besides those two immutables, in front of her at all times were the shifting daily challenges and ordeals: the dust storms, hailstones, sandflies, lurking snakes and scorpions, xenophobic border guards, and hostile provincial bureaucrats. There were thieves and bandits, as well, and even the occasional gun-wielding attacker—and always, always, those grueling, exhilarating miles. She describes it this way:

"Had I flown direct from Dublin and landed in Kabul as a wide-eyed newcomer to the East, I might well have been unable to appreciate the finer points of Afghan life and culture. As it is, during my two months of bicycling from Istanbul to Meshed, the roads became less road-like…the Moslems more Islamic, the sanitary arrangements more alarming…and the food dirtier. By the time I arrived at the Afghan frontier it seemed quite natural, before a meal, to scrape the dried mud off the bread, pick the hairs out of the cheese and remove the bugs from the sugar. I had also stopped registering the presence of fleas, the absence of cutlery, and the fact that I hadn't taken off my clothes or slept in a bed for ten days."

THE OCCASION HAD BEEN HER TENTH birthday, and somehow she had connected in her imagination the bicycle her parents had given her (the first she'd ever owned) to the distant lands depicted in the atlas sent by her grandfather.

"If I went on [bicycling] for long enough I could get to India," she realized, while speeding down the familiar Black-water Valley roads of her childhood. Yet, thrilled as she was, Dervla instinctively kept her new awareness, with its implicit promise, to herself. An only child, she was quite accustomed to the pleasures of private fantasies. To her, what she intended one day to accomplish seemed in no way extraordinary but, rather, completely logical. "I thought then, as I still do," she would explain patiently, "that if someone enjoys cycling and wishes to go to India, the obvious thing is to cycle there."

THE FROZEN FRENCH LANDSCAPE that surrounded her two decades later as she was about to launch herself, astride Roz, from Dunkirk into the unknown—destination New Delhi—was dismaying. Grim as the winter roads were, the temperatures were even more punishing. However, to Dervla, who'd grown up in a household where there had been a continual struggle to make ends meet, such obstacles seemed minor. She was no stranger to physical hardship, so it would have been difficult for anything so trivial as bad weather to dampen her spirits. After an increasingly claustrophobic young womanhood spent putting her parents' needs before her own, she was, following their deaths, suddenly free to do as she wished.

In fact, so delicious was her new liberty that, as she put it, "to be able unrestrainedly to gratify my wanderlust, after so many years of frustration, was all that mattered."

Thus, the frigid air was no deterrent, despite the tears she wept from the agony of the cold stabbing her fingers. Underway at last, she was more than ready simply to accept the unforeseen, along with its possible discomforts, as part of the psychic scenery.

"BEGIN AS YOU MEAN TO GO ON." It's a well-known maxim, and intentionally or not, one that Dervla Murphy adopted as her own. Thus, all of her subsequent expeditions over the next 35 years—whether through sub-Saharan Africa, the Carpathian Mountains, the Peruvian Andes, the Madagascar interior, or to any number of other exotic locales—were based on principles of simplicity and preparation established on that six-month-long maiden journey.

In the book describing that first trip, *Full Tilt : Ireland to India With a Bicycle*, she wrote, "The further you travel the less you find you need and I [saw] no sense in frolicking around the Himalayas with a load of inessentials."

AMONG THE BELONGINGS SHE CARRIED with her were a single, partial change of clothes (including woolen ankle-length underpants); a pair of fur-lined leather gloves and a face-covering balaclava helmet; one hundred water-purifying tablets; three tubes of insect repellent and six of sunscreen; a quantity of malaria pills; one camping knife; one thermos; and crucial spare parts for Roz.

Also deemed essential was an edition of the poems of William Blake. She did not carry an odometer, since, as she has said, "gadgets for measuring mileage" are of little use on roads barely worthy of the name.

Tibetan children look on from an Indian refugee camp as Dervla Murphy poses in 1963 with her first "mount," the bicycle she lovingly dubbed Rozinante, after the famed nag ridden by Cervantes' wandering Don Quixote.

On that original inventory was a .25 automatic pistol that she stowed in the pocket of her trousers, an item that proved its value early on. Back in Ireland assembling her gear, Dervla had chosen to ignore the mockery of friends who viewed its purchase as "so much adolescent melodrama." These scoffers, however, were safe at home when the foresightful Dervla was set upon by starving wolves in a dark Yugoslavian forest!

This terrifying assault occurred without any warning and was foiled only when, acting on nerves alone ("sheer panic," she says), Dervla succeeded in quickly pulling out her gun and shooting two of the three beasts at close range. As she wryly notes, she had "always thought there was something faintly comical in the idea of being devoured by wolves." Not so amusing, however, was the fact that one of the animals, prior to its untimely demise, had been hanging by its teeth off her shoulder, while the other, most unpleasantly, had attached itself to her ankle.

IN FACT, IT WASN'T LONG BEFORE DERVLA found herself having to produce her pistol once again—only the next time it happened, she was scaring off a wolf of a very different stripe.

In a cheap rooming house in Turkish Azerbaijan, she reports, "I awoke to find myself bereft of bedding and to see a six-foot, scantily-clad Kurd bending over me in the moonlight. My gun was beneath the pillow and one shot fired at the ceiling concluded the matter. I felt afterwards that my suitor had showed up rather badly; a more ardent admirer, of his physique, could probably have disarmed me without much difficulty."

Before Dervla Murphy ever traveled abroad, she had an intense appreciation of the countryside where she grew up. "There are profound differences between one's responses to familiar and unfamiliar landscapes. The incomparable grandeur of the Himalaya fills me with a mixture of exaltation and humility. But the beauty of the Blackwater valley is so much a part of me that it inspires an absurd pride—almost as though I had helped make it, instead of the other way around."

Dervla's father had been the county librarian for Lismore, and, accordingly, her girlhood was one filled with books. The family lived on his modest salary in what she has depicted as a dilapidated semidetached house little redeemed by its location on the town's "most respectable street."

In her memoir, *Wheels Within Wheels* (1979), Dervla powerfully evoked the aura of that cracked and peeling household. From the time she was three, her mother, owing to rheumatoid arthritis, was "a complete cripple, unable even to walk from the sitting-room to the downstairs lavatory, or to wash or dress herself." One can only speculate on the relation this tragedy bore to her daughter's compulsion to explore the world's more difficult terrains, relying almost entirely on the strength of her own legs. Yet equally relevant is the fact that from a very early age Dervla, encouraged by her parents, exhibited a desire not just to read books but also to write them.

For Christmas and birthday gifts she began early on to present her mother and father with long stories she had written. She summarizes the plot of one of these efforts:

"In about three thousand misspelled words it describes the adventures of two boys in a jungle that, judging by the available fauna, extended from Peru to Siberia. Having throttled a saber-toothed tiger with their bare hands, rescued a shepherd's baby from a condor and killed an anaconda with a poisoned dart, my heroes returned to Ireland by an unspecified route and lived happily ever after."

This effort, written when she was eight, sounds like nothing so much as typical episodes from her later life.

As SHE VENTURED BEYOND LISMORE and the Blackwater Valley and began to roam the world herself, Dervla, in the time-honored fashion of other literary globe-trotters, kept travel diaries and sent off letters that later would help provide supplementary material for her written accounts. Wearing her journal in a special pouch around her neck ("I never take it off"), she took to keeping a carbon with her and posting the top copy to friends.

In 1964, after she had returned to Ireland from India, she had cause to celebrate when the distinguished London publishing house of John Murray—who had given a literary home to Isabella Bird Bishop a century earlier—agreed to make Dervla one of its authors. The euphoric visit to their offices caused her such distraction that, despite surviving the hazards of cycling to India, she barely missed being run over by a bus!

THOUGH HER JOURNEYINGS have obviously been strenuous on every level, her genial stoicism, ironic intelligence, and temperamental inclination to wonder always "what's all the fuss about?" have made reading about them irresistible armchair diversion. The more outrageous the episode, the better the entertainment value, and Dervla's dry recitals—whether of being led astray by malicious monkeys in Pakistan, of vaulting across a Peruvian ravine into a stinging cactus, of trying to coax an ailing Malagasy minibus into action, or frantically searching for a lost packhorse in an underpopulated mountain region of Cameroon—have a soothingly addictive quality.

And, as forthrightly as Dervla had shaped her life as a solitary wanderer, so, in 1973 did she slide, with what seems wonderful ease, into her new role of single-globe-trotter-with-child. Her daughter, Rachel, who'd been born in 1968, was now old enough, she judged, to share with her peripatetic parent the stimulating effects of a journey beyond Europe's boundaries. So, after much debate over the best destination, India, a country she already knew, won out over Mexico. She explained the choice: "If travel is to be more than a relaxing break, or a fascinating job, the traveler's interest, enthusiasm, and curiosity must be reinforced by an emotional conviction that at present there is only one place worth visiting."

ONLY A DECADE EARLIER Dervla had headed across the English Channel on a ferry with a bicycle in tow; this time she was en route from Heathrow with a young human companion. Yet as their plane rose in the air, she understood now that she was to be fully engaged by a different sort of challenge: the responsibility of overseeing Rachel's "apprenticeship to serious traveling."

As *On a Shoestring to Coorg* (1977) relates, the four months they spent together in India would prove the start of a splendidly harmonious, occasionally slapstick, always loving partnership. It allowed Dervla's readers to watch her daughter, whose first mini-backpack contained such "luxuries" as a favorite stuffed squirrel and crayons, grow up.

"The Coorg trip was designed to test Rachel's' traveling capability," Dervla has explained. "She managed so well that a year later I decided she could cope with my very favorite sort of trek. So a few days after her sixth birthday we began our Baltistan journey—one of the toughest I have ever done. Rachel rode a retired polo pony and I walked. At night the temperature dropped to 40°F, and for three months we never took off our clothes. Food was scarce and we lived mainly on the Indian bread nan—which I cooked on a portable kerosene stove—and dried apricots. To this day, Rachel cannot stand the sights of apricots."

After this trip through Pakistan's Karakoram mountain range in 1974 (also explored by Fanny Bullock Workman), they next ventured into the Peruvian Andes when Rachel was nearly ten. *Eight Feet in the Andes*, (1983), was the result of this South American "frolic," and that expedition's continuous diet of mainly sardines caused Rachel to swear off them, as well.

On the trip immortalized in *Muddling Through Madagascar*, Rachel was 14. When they toured *Cameroon with Egbert* (1989), a Fulani stallion, she was a young adult of 18. *South from the Limpopo: Travels Through South Africa* (1997), Rachel Murphy was working on her own in Mozambique and found herself called upon to help smuggle her mother into the country, when the proper visa was held up by the local bureaucracy.

"Never mind," Dervla says her daughter, in genuine chip-off-the-old-block fashion, told her, when she learned of her mother's unexpected delay. "There's a smuggler's path over the mountains on the border. If you sneak in that way, before dawn, we'll pick you up on the far side. But remember the land mines, don't ever leave the path. If you need to pee, pee on the path."

DERVLA MURPHY, STILL TRAVELING, and just returned from Serbia, (she describes it, tersely, as "quite sad"), is now the proud grandmother of three. As a person who has long publicly confessed her need for solitude, she's also a woman who understands from experience how "small children form links, not barriers." One imagines, then, that it won't be long before one of Rachel's children, filled with excitement and carrying a small knapsack, will be ready to join Dervla and take to the beckoning road. ■

AIRBORNE

AMELIA EARHART   1897 – 1937

SHANNON LUCID   1943 –

Stars hung outside my cockpit

window near enough to touch.

I have never seen so many or

such large ones.

I shall never forget the contrast

of the white clouds and

the moonlight and starlight against

the black of the sea...."

AMELIA EARHART
1897 – 1937

"AT NO TIME DURING THE FLIGHT did the outside temperature register below 40° F. However, I had the cockpit window open a bit and the cold rain beat in on me until I became thoroughly chilled. I thought it would be rather pleasant to have a cup of hot chocolate. So I did and it was. Indeed that was the most interesting cup of chocolate I have ever had, sitting up 8,000 feet over the middle of the Pacific Ocean, quite alone."

THE PLANE IN WHICH AMELIA EARHART was soloing

across the Pacific in January 1935, while she contentedly sipped cocoa up in the clouds, was a single-engine Lockheed-Vega. Almost three years before, in May 1932, she had successfully flown across the Atlantic alone—the first woman do so—piloting an almost identical craft. This time her route was taking her from Hawaii to California, and she was in the process of setting another record.

The little Lockheed-Vega was a plane she loved—"my companion aloft for so many flying hours." Its very paint scheme, bright red with gold stripes, appeared delightful to her. "Possibly it may have seemed a trifle gaudy on the ground but I am sure it looked lovely against one of those white clouds," she would later write, fondly recalling its bold style.

Flying eastward through the Pacific night in 1935, this boyishly attractive woman, her face by then recognizable the world over, was a veteran pilot of 15 years' standing. The flight that had made her a public personage had taken place seven years earlier, when she'd been offered the chance to be the first woman aboard a three-person transatlantic flight.

Noisily greeted upon her return from that original crossing with parades and celebrations across America, she quickly had been dubbed "Lady Lindy" by enthusiastic headline writers. It was, of course, a way of linking her triumph—which she herself regarded as overrated, since she'd been obliged by prior agreement to let the pilot and flight mechanic do all the work—to that of Charles Lindbergh, the legendary transatlantic hero of a year earlier.

AMELIA HAD TAKEN THE CONTROLS of her very first Lockheed-Vega in 1928. It was with high anticipation that she intended to fly it in what she knew to be the historic occasion of the first women's cross-country air derby. Yet, despite being purchased thirdhand and quite a bit the worse for the wear, her new possession still seemed to her to be a 'heavenly chariot.'

But, before the contest, she decided to take a spin from New York to California, where, as a precautionary measure, she'd have it checked out by experts at the Lockheed factory. What they told her, and what she hadn't been expecting to hear, was that she was lucky to have arrived there in one piece, because of the plane's worn and missing parts.

But, until the old Lockheed was traded for a brand new one, the best part, according to Amelia, was hearing the general amazement at her seat-of-the-pants flying skills. "The fact that I could herd such a hopeless piece of mechanism across the continent successfully was the one bright spot in the ensuing half hour."

FOR A.E., AS SHE WAS TO BE KNOWN, flying was the ultimate magnetic force, its power strong enough to compel her to work long hours as unskilled labor sorting mail in order to pay for her first bright yellow plane.

Whenever she would tell the story of how she came to her calling, she would explain that it had its origins in a stint as a nurse's aide that she'd idealistically undertaken in Toronto in during World War I. It had been there, when she was 20 years old, that she'd met and admired a group of dashing young military pilots. The glamorous aura they gave off—it was, after all, "the romantic branch of the service," as she noted—so infected her that soon she could dream only of learning to fly herself.

But first she would enroll in medical school at Columbia University and put in time doing "the peculiar things they do who would be physicians." It was a fine plan for someone, just not for Amelia, for she found she could no more forget airplanes than she could happily sit in a lab and dissect cockroaches.

"Aviation had come close to me" is the oddly phrased and haunting explanation she gives in her first book, *20 Hrs, 40 Min.*, as a way of describing the lingering effects of that Canadian sojourn. However, all that meant was now she had a desire to bring it even closer. During her very first ride, with a barnstormer named Frank Hawks, she had left the ground behind for only a few hundred feet before realizing what she'd already intuitively known—that she was born to fly.

IN TRUTH, THE FIRST AIRPLANE that Amelia Mary Earhart, daughter of a railroad man, had ever seen was one on display at the Iowa State Fair when she was ten. "It was a thing of rusty wire and wood and looked not at all interesting."

A well-meaning adult pointed out, "Look, dear, it flies," attempting to stimulate her curiosity about the strange contraption. But Amelia, her stubborn juvenile attention elsewhere, wasn't at the time having any of it.

Only a decade later, however, she would avidly seek initiation into the society of air jockeys and stunt pilots, looking to make herself at home in the shacks and hangars of the dusty airfields of the day. Yet, exciting as was her new milieu, even she quickly realized to what extent the world of flight was still in its frontier period.

Formal instruction was almost nonexistent, and such bureaucratic niceties as licenses were not yet required. (Amelia's own pilot's license, she claimed, was the first granted to an American woman by the the Fédération Aéronautique Internationale. At airfields everywhere, an anything-goes atmosphere prevailed. (This meant, in practice, that it was perfectly okay for anyone to *go* anywhere.) "Pilots landed in pastures, race courses, even golf links where they were still enough of a novelty to be welcome," Amelia would recall. And while not an environment entirely closed to women, flying was still, according to Amelia, "pretty well a man-conducted business."

At times it even appeared, really, more of "a jumble of gallant individual efforts" than anything that could properly be called an industry. Yet, the intensity of Amelia's dedication, along with her growing skill—and, of course, her nerve, became apparent in situations such as she describes below.

"FOR THOSE FIRST HOURS I WAS flying at about 12,000 feet. And then something happened that has never occurred in my 12 years of flying. The altimeter, the instrument that records height above the ground, failed. Suddenly the hands swung around the dial uselessly and I knew the instrument was out of commission for the rest of the flight.

"About 11:30, the moon disappeared behind some clouds, and I ran into rather a severe storm with lightning, and I was considerably buffeted about, and with difficulty held my course…. This lasted for an hour. Then I flew on in calmer weather though in the midst of clouds. Once I saw the moon for a fleeting instant and thought I could pull out on the top of the clouds, so I climbed for half an hour when suddenly I realized I was picking up ice.

"I knew by the climb of the ship, which was not as fast as usual, that it was accumulating a weight of ice. Then I saw slush on the windowpane. In addition, my tachometer, the instrument that registers revolutions per minute of the motor, picked up ice and spun around the dial....

"I descended until I could see the waves breaking, although I could not tell exactly how far I was above them. I kept flying here until fog came down so low that I dared not keep on at such an altitude...."

As AMELIA EARHART ROSE FROM obscurity to international renown, nothing would ever matter to her as much as the unbeatable exhilaration and pure *fun* of rising thousands of feet in the air. Even when the wings were iced and there were flames erupting from her engine or her gas reserves leaking, as had all occurred on her first solo transatlantic flight, Amelia was happy. So it is no surprise that she chose to title her second book, published in 1932, *The Fun of It: Random Records of My Own Flying and of Women in Aviation*.

Nonetheless, "I didn't like public flying," she wrote, although it would soon comprise the largest part of her airborne existence. Initially, at any rate, she had an innate distaste for feeding the mass audience's bottomless appetite for sensation.

"It didn't coincide with my ideas of what I wished to do with my plane. It was hard enough to keep out of the papers anyway in those days if one flew. The slightest mishap was called a crash and disasters were played up lugubriously."

For herself, she insisted, "flying was a sport and not a circus—I used to sneak to a secluded field and practice with no one to bother. I appeared in public only on special occasions."

Unfortunately, after the enormous continuing stream of attention that overtook her following the 1928 transatlantic flight—public scrutiny that would become even more frenzied with the notoriety following her 1932 solo crossing of the Atlantic—Amelia's independence, valued above all else, was under siege. But she attempted to balance the demands being made upon her with the life she craved to lead.

Fortunately, perhaps the most importunate of those new friends laying claim to her attention was the wealthy publisher George Palmer Putnam, who'd been one of the men to vet her for the opportunity to make her historic transatlantic flight aboard the *Friendship*. After she had turned down his first five proposals of marriage, unsure if such a commitment could be reconciled with the personal freedom she sought, she did a turnabout, and without warning, accepted his sixth.

It was to be Putnam, though, whose supportive interest in his second wife's already extraordinary career would make it possible for her to continue the personal flight path she'd begun charting.

AT BREAKFAST ONE MORNING EARLY in 1932, at their house in Rye, New York, Amelia is supposed to have asked George a question that only a new husband married to a record-making "aviatrix" might have any right to expect.

Would he have any objections, she wondered, if she now prepared to fly the Atlantic alone? His reply was to invite to lunch another experienced flyer, the Norwegian pilot Bernt Balchen, who, by the end of the meal, had signed on as technical adviser.

By the beginning of April, Amelia still had not yet informed her mother of her plans even though Mrs. Earhart's encouragement had never faltered in the past— she had even helped A. E. buy her first plane. Yet, Amelia was every day determinedly plunging ahead, assisted by her husband and Balchen, working out every detail toward an imminent departure.

By the middle of May, all systems were go, and local weather conditions were being scrutinized for the most advantageous departure. On May 20, the day the go-ahead came from George, who remained in constant contact with a senior meteorologist, Amelia was caught unprepared. Needing to rush back to Rye for necessities, she was ruthlessly efficient: "Five minutes was enough to pick up my things," she later wrote.

Bernt Balchen would wind up accompanying her from her home field in New Jersey to Harbor Grace, Newfoundland. There, on May 21, a few minutes past seven in the evening, wearing jodhpurs and a wind-breaker under her leather flying suit, Amelia Earhart heard a last message relayed from her husband, shook hands with Balchen and her mechanic, climbed into the cockpit of her Vega monoplane, and "gave her the gun."

In 1932, Amelia Earhart touched down in an Irish meadow after nearly 15 hours of flight. She then stopped at a nearby farm-house to wash her face, drink some tea, and sign an autograph.

From then on, she was utterly and entirely on her own.

AFTER COPING WITH A STEADY series of technical difficulties—the final two hours of the nearly 15-hour flight were the hardest, she wrote, what with the gas leak and a near-complete lack of visibility—Amelia landed in an Irish meadow.

Sticking her head out of the cockpit, she acknowledged her greeters, three surprised people who emerged from the nearby farmhouse, by informing them cheerfully, "I'm from America."

A TRULY AMERICAN HEROINE, Amelia Earhart, for this trail-blazing 20th-century accomplishment (she was also the first person to cross the Atlantic twice) was awarded, among many honors, the Harmon International Trophy, the United States Congress' Distinguished Flying Cross, the cross of the French Legion of Honor, and the Special Gold Medal of the National Geographic Society.

At the banquet in Washington where she received this last tribute, following a formal White House dinner with President Hoover and Mrs. Hoover, she was modest about her success in the face of the occasion's rampant adulation.

She preferred, instead, to acknowledge the contribution of Bernt Balchen ("any expedition owes 60 percent of its success to the preparation beforehand") and to hope that the flight would further the cause of transatlantic air travel, as well as forwarding the cause of women in aviation.

Finally, she promised her listeners, who were hanging on her every word, that, contrary to rumors, she hadn't killed any Irish cows on landing—"unless one died of fright."

AMELIA EARHART, IN HER DASHING and inspirational 17-year air career, set 13 important records, from being the first woman to solo the continental United States roundtrip (1928) to being the first person to solo over the Pacific (1935). She broke the women's nonstop transcontinental speed record twice (1932 and 1933), and she was in the midst of a flight around the world, on her most daring, record-shattering adventure yet, when her plane disappeared near Howland Island, in the equatorial waters of the central Pacific.

IN THE BOOK *Last Flight* (1937), working primarily from the flight notes, log records, and letters she'd cabled back to him, George Putnam assembled the poignant trajectory of his wife's unfinished journey. Amelia, he wrote, had often contemplated her chances of survival as she looked out at the sea before her departure. "It's a very big ocean—so much water!" he says she once remarked with a sigh.

But whatever happened, she had always been clear on one crucial point: "When I go, I'd like best to go in my plane. Quickly." ■

"I floated [in front of Mir's]
large observation window and
gazed at the earth below....
Invariably, I was struck by
the majesty of the unfolding scene.
The most amazing thing of all was
that here I was, a child of the
pre-Sputnik, Cold War 1950s,
living on a
Russian space station."

SHANNON LUCID
1943 -

"**D**URING MY EARLY CHILDHOOD in the Texas Panhandle, I had spent a significant amount of time chasing wind-blown tumbleweeds across the prairie. Now I was in a vehicle that resembled a cosmic tumbleweed, working and socializing with a Russian air force officer and Russian engineer. Just ten years ago such a plot line would have been deemed too implausible for anything but a science-fiction novel."

Even before American astronaut Shannon Wells Lucid had traveled a record-setting 89 million miles in space, her life was no ordinary one. The daughter of a evangelical Baptist missionary, she had spent the first years of her childhood in China, on the other side of the globe she was later to orbit.

Her family, during World War II, after enduring the frightening uncertainties of almost a year's internment in a Japanese concentration camp, was fortunate enough to be among those ordered released under the terms of a negotiated prisoners exchange. Having left the country aboard the historic rescue ship, the S.S. *Gripsholm*, the Wellses, once the war had ended, did succeed in returning to their Chinese mission. But by 1949, they were forced once again to forsake it, with the establishment of the People's Republic of China and communist rule—only this time their exile was permanent.

Yet for Shannon, who had spent all but six weeks of her first year of life in an internment camp, and who had already been around the world twice before turning six, her earliest significant memory is not one that draws on the exotic Asian landscape. Rather, she carries with her a mental snapshot evoking a more prosaic Michigan scene: herself, tirelessly pulling a little red wagon during a trip home to visit relatives.

Trudging on with wagon in tow, obviously completely absorbed in her journey, she would catch the attention of passing adults, some of whom stopped to inquire, kindly, where she thought she was going. The grandness of the answer she says she gave does seem a presentiment of the career to come: "I told them I wanted to explore the world."

Not long after that, the young Shannon, lacking any proof of the matter, stubbornly refused to believe the outrageous grown-up claim that when it was night in the United States it was daytime in China. Deciding this was something she'd simply have to prove to her own satisfaction, she set out one day, prepared to walk around the world to determine whether such a disturbing nugget of information could possibly be true.

"I told my mother, and she just said, 'you go ahead, dear.'" It was only hours later, after frantically searching for her, that her worried parents found their budding scientist asleep curled up on a rock.

Her interests weren't always so earthbound, however. From a tender age, she was equally intrigued by every sort of air travel. For example, when flying from Shanghai to the cool mountain village where her family went to escape the city's heat, she was delighted, she recalls, with each opportunity to watch their descent from the window of the unpressurized converted army aircraft. "I'd see the gravel strip below and the thought would come to me that this was the most incredible thing, to be able to fly, to land the plane."

Once resettled in the States and attending a Texas elementary school in the early 1950s, Shannon Wells' imagination suddenly began to take flight in new directions. Although she had often accompanied her father (who was a preacher) by train, bus, and automobile, Shannon now sought not only to fly, but also to soar past our own atmosphere. She wanted to explore the vastness of space that lay beyond it.

She was a little girl ahead of her time. And not only had she started fantasizing about it decades before she herself would come to arrive triumphantly in space, but, as she likes to point out, she was onto the idea long in advance of the existence of any government space program.

Thus, her indignation still is evident when she describes how she felt as a space-obsessed teenaged girl in 1959, after learning that the first seven Apollo astronauts selected by the recently created National Aeronautics and Space Administration were all men. (At her Oklahoma high school, "gym wasn't even for girls. You were supposed to be in the pep club and cheer. I was the only girl not a member of the pep club. I wanted to take shop, but, no way, it was a futile effort.")

Still, knowing how the system operated did nothing to make the frustrations any less real, or to make her feel any less bitter. The NASA announcement, Shannon says, was at the time her "most devastating experience," and, in protest, she even sat down and wrote a letter to *Time* that gave voice to her anger. (In the years 1960 and 1963, NASA was to reject for astronaut training three women recommended to the program, despite their having met the qualifications.)

ONCE GRADUATED FROM THE UNIVERSITY of Oklahoma with a degree in chemistry in 1963, Shannon went on to complete her advanced studies there, as well, earning her doctorate in biochemistry in 1973. Throughout her years of graduate work, she had consistently found academic and laboratory jobs. Now, with Ph.D. in hand, she was hired as a research associate in 1974 by the Oklahoma Medical Research Foundation, where some years earlier she'd toiled as a senior lab technician.

This position, though well-suited to her professional credentials, was not what her heart dictated as first choice. "I had gotten my pilot's license by then, but I couldn't get any kind of flying job. They weren't hiring females, period."

But as the laws of the land had begun to change regarding sexual discrimination, so was NASA on the brink of transforming itself. Soon enough rumors were starting to circulate in the scientific community that the next class of astronauts selected would be a coed one. That was all Shannon Wells Lucid needed to know. For, even though she had married her husband, Michael, in 1968, and was busy as the mother of three children, she had never ceased to keep a watchful eye on her ultimate dream job. The year was 1977.

"I sent my application in, and then there was about a week's worth of medical tests and interviews," is how she modestly portrays the extraordinarily selective process that saw her accepted into the Class of '78. (Sally Ride, another of the six women among the 35 classmates, would become, in 1983, the very first American woman to go into space.)

A little more than a year and a half after joining her astronaut class, Shannon Lucid had qualified for assignment as a mission specialist on space shuttle flight crews. But it would be a very busy six years on the ground—working in Mission Control, as well as on other aspects of critical technical and administrative support—before an assignment to the shuttle *Discovery* provided, finally, in June of 1985, her long-awaited passport to the stars.

SHANNON LUCID HAS SAID, " You could live in a padded room if you wanted to, but that wouldn't be much of a life." A padded uniform, on the other hand, is very much worth having, especially if one's wearing it at the behest of the United States government 240 miles out in space.

Four years later, after her STS-51G *Discovery*

mission, Shannon joined the crew of the shuttle STS-34 *Atlantis,* which, among other tasks performed over five days in space, deployed the Galileo spacecraft on its way to explore Jupiter. Then, not quite two years after that 1989 mission had made its landing at Edwards Air Force Base in California, she was launched on the STS-43 *Atlantis* for 9 days and 142 orbits of the Earth; during this flight, the astronauts on board conducted numerous experiments and deployed a Tracking and Data Relay Satellite.

By the time she had completed her next assignment—orbiting Earth 225 times on the Spacelab STS-58 *Columbia* in 1993 (its human crew, along with the 48 rats on board, gained NASA recognition for the "most successful and efficient Spacelab flight")—Shannon Lucid was not just a seasoned veteran, but a bona fide record holder.

The 838 hours and 54 minutes she had by then logged on her four NASA missions made her the premier American woman space traveler, and she wasn't finished yet.

"Based on my own experience, I believe that there are several lessons that should be applied to the operation of the International Space Station. First, the station crew must be chosen carefully. Even if the space station has the latest in futuristic technology, if the crew does not enjoy working together, the flight will be a miserable experience. Second, NASA must recognize that a long-duration flight is as different from a shuttle flight as a marathon is from a 100-yard dash. On a typical two-week shuttle flight, NASA ground controllers assign every moment of the crew's time to some task. But the crew on a long-duration flight must be treated more like scientists in a laboratory on the Earth. They must have some control over their daily schedules."

Following three months of intensive Russian-language study and then a full year at Star City, the Russian cosmonaut training center outside Moscow, Shannon Lucid, at the end of March 1996, was ready to join her crewmates, Commander Yuri Onufriyenko and flight engineer Yuri Usachev, who had preceded her to *Mir*.

Lifting off from Kennedy Space Center on the shuttle *Atlantis*, she spent three days in transit from coastal Florida to the Russian space station that was speeding continuously around the Earth at 17,000 miles an hour.

Because the two Yuris spoke no English, Shannon—who, though she considers herself "language compromised," had mastered technical Russian—had to meet them on their own turf in more ways than the most obvious one. The joys of cultural exchange in space included learning to enjoy their dehydrated borscht while watching her companions happily add packets of American mayonnaise to nearly everything they ate.

Housekeeping chores took up a part of each day, as the trio collected trash, kept their food supply organized, and sponged up water that would collect on cool surfaces. Regular exercise, too, was a strictly observed daily ritual, as, in harness and with bungee cords, they performed treadmill and strength-maintaining routines that had been specially designed for gravity-less space conditions by Russian physiologists.

When she was ready each night to turn in, Shannon's first order of business was to secure her sleeping bag to a fixed railing, in order that she might "wake up in more or less the same spot every morning." Sleeping ten inches off the ground, however, was no problem. "At midnight," she has written, "I turned out the light and floated into my sleeping bag. I always slept soundly until the alarm went off the next morning." Shannon Lucid wound up billeted on *Mir* for far longer than had been scheduled, outlasting even her original Russian partners. Her expected ride home to Earth was six weeks late arriving, and she found herself on hold while NASA engineers worked to adjust the booster rockets on *Atlantis*. (She has remarked that, informed of the delay, she only saw it as a hardship once she realized the extra hours she'd be forced to put in tethered to the treadmill.)

The experiments she made while traveling more than 75,000,000 miles in *Mir* included studying the effects of microgravity on the embryonic development of fertilized Japanese quail eggs. "I was living every scientist's dream. I had my own lab and worked independently for much of the day. Before one experiment became dull, it was time to start another, with new equipment and in a new scientific field…. I believe my experience on *Mir* clearly shows the value of performing research on manned space stations. During some of the experiments, I was able to observe subtle phenomena that a video or still camera would miss. Because I was familiar with the science in each experiment, I could sometimes examine the results on the spot and modify the procedures as needed."

However, since the fixative solution presented a potential safety hazard should a drop have escaped—it could have floated into a crew member's eye and caused severe burns—she worked with the eggs contained in a series of interlocking clear bags. All of the bags were enclosed in a bigger sack with gloves attached to it, enabling Shannon to manipulate her samples with the seal intact.

Afloat on the Russian space station Mir, *Shannon Lucid
poses for a patriotic Fourth of July photograph.
In 1996, she spent 188 weightless days in
cramped conditions she fondly describes as not unlike
"those of a family camper on a rainy day."*

In microgravity experiments in space, she explains, you have the chance to "remove that one constant, Earth's gravity, and it allows you to see what that particular factor affects, does or doesn't change."

"Many of our experiments provided useful data for the engineers designing the International Space Station. The results from our investigations in fluid physics are helping the space station's planners build better ventilation and life-support systems. And our research on how flames propagate in microgravity may lead to improved procedures for fighting fires on the station."

For Lucid, who urges future space station occupants to be certain they have a hobby before they lift off, reading was her own choice of leisure activity when she wasn't sharing jokes or tea and cookies with Onufriyenko and Usachev. "I never get enough of flying or of reading books," she avows. And so she happily devoured 50 volumes during the months on *Mir*, having made sure one of her daughters would keep her stocked in space with novels that had plenty of "words per page." (The personally selected packets of fresh literature arrived in two batches during Shannon's stay, as part of the cargo carried by one of the unmanned supply vessels that would dock with *Mir* every few months.)

"I told her to pick out books she knew I hadn't read, and so I wound up with Dickens, as well as lots of 17th- and 18th-century authors...after a while, I was definitely ready for something a bit more modern."

"I DISCOVERED THAT DURING A LONG spaceflight, as opposed to a quick space shuttle jaunt, I could see the flow of seasons across the face of the globe. When I arrived on

Mir at the end of March, the higher latitudes of the Northern Hemisphere were covered with ice and snow. Within a few weeks, though, I could see huge cracks in the lakes as the ice started to break up. Seemingly overnight, the Northern Hemisphere glowed green with spring."

Despite spending more hours in space than any other American to date, Shannon Lucid has hardly had her fill of either its demands or its wonders. She may have described conditions aboard *Mir* as similar to being "in a camper in the back of your pickup with your kids…when it's raining and no one can get out," but it doesn't mean she wouldn't gladly go back again in an instant.

In late 1999, not yet having given up on her chance for a sixth space shuttle assignment or possibly even a berth on board the new International Space Station, she has noticed with some amusement that her now-adult children stand ready to wave her off again. "They say: 'It's about time. We're getting tired of having you hang around the house all the time just thinking about wanting to fly in space.'"

Just as they did when she was small, those thoughts of space continue to engage Shannon's imagination, almost at an addictive level. "It's why I stay here in the office [in the Lyndon B. Johnson Space Center, in Houston]. I'd love to go back. The problem is," she sighs, "there are lots of us, all with the same idea."

But, of course, not all of them are Shannon Lucids. President Clinton called her "a determined visionary" as he presented her with the Congressional Space Medal of Honor at a White House ceremony in 1996. She was the first woman ever to receive this elite distinction, which marks accomplishment beyond the ordinary boundaries of even the most extreme—but earthbound—adventurers. ■

ON
ASSIGNMENT

HARRIET CHALMERS ADAMS
1875-1937

SYLVIA A. EARLE
1935-

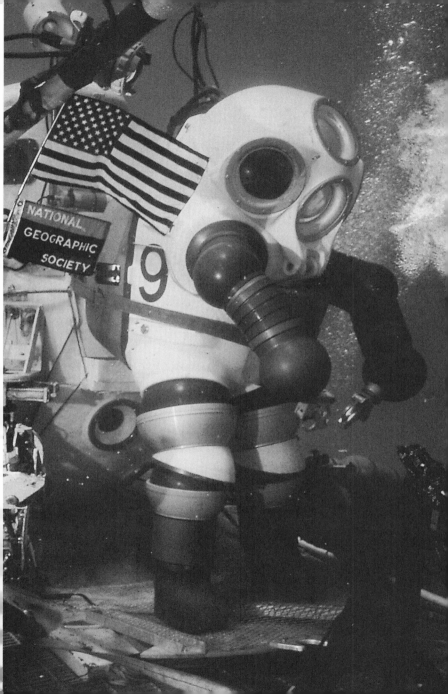

"I've never found my sex

a hinderment;

never faced a difficulty which

a woman, as well as man,

could not surmount;

never felt fear of danger;

never lacked courage to protect myself.

I've been in tight places,

and have seen harrowing things."

HARRIET CHALMERS ADAMS
1875 – 1937

"WE ALL HAVE A MECCA. It is New York, for one; for another, Paris. Some people long to reach the Holy Land. Since childhood I had journeyed in my dreams on the long pilgrimage to Cuzco, and when I at last found myself in the Andean country, on that portion of the old Inca highway stretching from Lake Titicaca to the "City of the Sun," I knew that sometimes dreams come true."

By the time those words were published in the October 1908 issue of NATIONAL GEOGRAPHIC,

California-born Harriet Chalmers Adams could claim, without the slightest exaggeration, to be a veteran traveler who had seen not just the City of the Sun, but much of Central and South America.

Her been-there-done-that litany ran the gamut from surviving a Bolivian earthquake, and skirting alligators and boa constrictors, to nearly dying from eating a cooked bird brought down by a poisoned arrow. She once even resorted to sheltering amid a pack of warm, wild llamas during a blizzard and afterward explained, "It was a bare mountain side without possibility of refuge or help...[but] I slept warm and comfortable."

Harriet also experienced a frightening run-in with vampire bats. Deep in a South American jungle one night, she thought she heard ominous noises while preparing for sleep. In her journal she wrote offhandedly, "I suppose those sounds come from jaguars playing tag about the house." But as daylight arrived, Harriet awoke to find her companions breathing raspingly, with blood visible on their heads, chests, and throats. As she bandaged their wounds, it became apparent that vampire bats had entered the hut, then attacked. Harriet herself had been spared only because she had drawn a veil protectively over her head before she slept.

HARRIET ADAMS WAS A 25-YEAR-OLD married woman when she ventured outside the United States for the first time in 1900 with her husband Frank at her side. During this trip, which was a delayed honeymoon spent in back-country Mexico, they had quickly gotten the hang of immersing themselves in local customs and difficult living conditions. The result of those early Mexican adventures was not only to reinforce her wanderlust, but also to instill in her the desire to substitute, within her marriage, the excitement of travel for the stability of home and hearth.

Why not, she urged Frank (whose work on an engineering survey had provided the original excuse for their venturing into Mexico), from now on seek only the sorts of jobs that might keep their suitcases permanently packed? More than willing to oblige, he looked around and came up with a proposal for a three-year stay in Latin America as well as South America, with a contract to inspect a far-flung series of mines. Harriet, overjoyed, immediately began to plan their itinerary.

Much later, when she could look back at a lifetime of such journeys, Harriet summed up the essence of her anti-domestic arrangements, saying: "Clothes become tattered, and shoes have a most annoying habit of wearing out; but the air and the sunlight, and the adventure and romance of exploration are full compensation to some of us for discomfort, hardship and danger."

HARRIET CHALMERS was born in 1875. Her hometown, Stockton, California, an inland seaport on the San Joaquin River, had earlier served as a supply center during the legendary gold rush days. Her father, Alexander, had himself first arrived in town as a prospector before settling down to the more respectable, less volatile business of running a dry goods store. It was he, an avid outdoorsman, who wielded the greatest power over his oldest child's development, ignoring at all times his wife Fannie's predictable maternal concern for her daughter's stamina and safety.

Just as Isabella Bird Bishop, four decades earlier,

had accompanied her clergyman father on horseback through the countryside, so did Harriet also have a papa who wished to have his daughter ride at his side. Harriet was reportedly was only two years old when the pair headed off for the first time into the Sierra Nevada mountain range.

Their first really ambitious outing, though, took place when Harriet was just eight. She and her father explored on horseback the Pacific coast, crossing California to Yosemite Falls, and traveling all the way to the Canadian Rockies. (Mrs. Chalmers and Harriet's younger sister, Anna, apparently preferred more sedate holidays at proper resorts.)

Both Harriet and Anna were by 1886 being educated by tutors at home. So the constraints of scheduled school hours offered no obstacle when, in the spring of 1889, Alexander Chalmers decided to embark with his favorite trail companion on a year-long ramble. As they ranged from the Oregon border down to Mexico, the 14-year-old Harriet instinctively knew she was having both an extraordinary experience and one that would send its echoes resounding throughout her life.

"I was an explorer when I was too young to realize it," she would later remark happily.

And if these trips "stirred powerfully" Harriet's already active imagination, she also, as a book-loving child, quite soon grasped that it lay within her not just to travel where she wished when she grew up but to envision that, one day, she also might write about her own adventures.

HARRIET WAS QUITE SMALL in stature and presented a

fetchingly feminine appearance; she was drawn to eye-catching hats and handsome clothes, even when she left civilization behind. (At one point, while trekking in the Andes, we know she packed, with the utmost security, a precious jar of cold cream.) Yet in Stockton, as she approached young womanhood, she remained tomboyish with a hometown reputation for physical prowess and courage.

If she climbed a tree, it had to be the highest; if she took up a sport, she strove to be the best at it. At the same time, she was a voracious reader and intellectually curious, with a natural gift for languages (she would eventually master Spanish, Portuguese, Italian, German, and French). And it was likely that it was this contrasting mixture of attributes, linked to such a free spirit, that attracted Franklin Adams to Harriet.

Seven years her senior and trained as an engineer, he was employed at the Stockton Gas and Electric Company, where his father was superintendent, when they began their courtship. At the time of their marriage, in 1899, Harriet and Frank shared dreams of far-off places. Yet, lacking funds, they had to settle, at first, for less ambitious jaunts around their home state. Now, Harriet would frequently pass beyond the Stockton city limits seated not astride a horse but next to Frank in an automobile, since both Adamses were quickly drawn to this new mode of transportation.

Under Frank's tutelage, Harriet began her apprenticeship in photography. When they left for Latin America in 1904, sailing out of San Francisco Bay, they carried with them a three years' supply of film and equipment, including a motion-picture camera. Their plan was to let Frank fulfill his business obligations, while Harriet would keep journals recording the sights and sounds of their wayfaring days.

Since she had read widely in preparation for this trip, she was thrilled to find how well her careful research research into the region's history connected with what they were actually seeing.

"As the train steamed away," she was to write, in another of her NATIONAL GEOGRAPHIC articles, "leaving us in the little Andean village of thatched mud huts, I pinched myself to make sure I was awake. We were in Tiahuanaco, an Indian hamlet, situated on that bleak upland plain of Bolivia [and] the departure of the train seemed to have dropped [us] back 500 years. 'No trace here of Spanish invasion,' I said; but just then we came upon a street shrine and a stone cross, and were reminded that these highland Indians are no longer sun-worshippers."

Harriet relished such triumphs as becoming the first woman to travel from the Amazon River to Cayenne, in French Guiana, and successfully gaining the summit of Peru's El Misti, with its elevation of more than 19,000 feet. And even after "long days in the saddle, with little food and less water" and only the ground to sleep on, she was always capable of projecting her own flights of fancy: "I was a Quichua princess carried by my willing slaves down to the beautiful summer palace of my father, the Inca."

That is, until reality intervened. "Only just then my tired horse stumbled, and I came back to earth a dusty little Andean traveler longing for any moth-eaten *posada* where I could rest my weary head."

WHEN THE ADAMSES ARRIVED BACK in the United States in mid-1906, there was some inevitable letdown. Frank's contract with the mining companies was fulfilled, and the next position he secured was on the East Coast, with the Bureau of American Republics (now the Pan American Union), a job that now would keep him relatively desk-bound in Washington, D.C.

This left Harriet with the challenge of finding outlets for the material she had so faithfully amassed (including at least three thousand photos) during the course of their Latin American and South American circuit. Earning money, too, was crucial if she meant, as she always had, never to stop traveling.

Boldly approaching the National Geographic Society, an organization 13 years younger than she, Harriet managed to intrigue, by the vivacity of her correspondence, the Society's president, Gilbert H. Grosvenor. At his invitation, she delivered her first Society-sponsored lecture that same year to an enthusiastic audience.

Soon, the success she enjoyed as a public speaker under the Society's auspices translated into demand from every sort of group, in all corners of the country, for Harriet's lively illustrated talks.

In 1911, with her reputation growing, she made use of her southern hemispheric expertise to address the assembled representatives of the Pan-American Commercial Conference on Latin American trade issues—and received from them a highly gratifying standing ovation. But even more significant for the 35-year-old Harriet was the honor of sharing a platform with President William Howard Taft.

As she started to contribute regularly to NATIONAL GEOGRAPHIC—21 articles in 28 years would be her total—

she based the first six of her published pieces on her observations from the 1904-1906 trip. And when finally she turned her efforts in a new direction for the Society, she did so rather spectacularly. In the 1917 November-December issue appears, "In French Lorraine: That Part of France Where the First American Soldiers Have Fallen," marking her debut as a war correspondent.

Harriet entered France in 1916, two years after World War I had begun. Determinedly waving around the "magical little yellow book" that contained her identity papers and magazine affiliation, she was the only woman journalist permitted to visit soldiers at the front lines and to take pictures of French battles.

In the town of Nancy, where she was based, she once found herself caught off guard by an enemy bombardment and forced into a cellar with 26 other people, a dog, and a pet canary. "I have never heard anything as ominous as the sound of those titanic shells," she wrote, "each crushing out homes and human beings…. We sat on boxes. There was a light, and over in one corner I saw a keg and a sack, evidently containing water and food; and a pickax.

"How, I wondered, could we dig our way out with that one pickax, should the house be struck…. By my wristwatch the shells fell every seven minutes. The bombardment lasted three-quarters of an hour, and we remained in the cellar for some time after the last crash, which sounded much nearer than the others."

LATER, WHEN HARRIET RETURNED home from France, she dedicated herself to raising money for the American Fund for the French Wounded. Paying her own expenses much of the time, she would speak passionately on her subject in as many as six small towns a day. Although she would vividly describe the war-torn landscape and battle casualties she had witnessed, she preferred to make little capital of her own near escape.

In fact, when asked whether she had been terrified to be that close to the shelling, she modestly explained that her temporary bravery counted for little "when thousands of French women are living in towns which are being constantly bombarded."

FROM 1909 ON, EVEN BEFORE SHE had sailed off to war, the mileage that Harriet logged was nothing short of dizzying. In that year she returned alone to South America to report for the Society on "The First Transandine Railroad from Buenos Aires to Valparaiso." Back in the States, she combined colorful anecdotes with photographs from her trip and once more captivated her audiences. For example, amused by the efforts of a Buenos Aires café proprietor to prepare for the heavy American tourist travel expected there that year because of the new railroad, she recalled the "glittering electric sign" he'd created after consultation with local British residents. "Fried Potatoes and Champagne" was the proud boast he hoped would lure new diners—and Harriet had the picture to prove it.

The following year she traveled with Frank to Cuba, Puerto Rico, Haiti, and the Dominican Republic, during which trip they triumphantly collected five *solenodons* from deep in the Haitian interior. (This small nocturnal mammal, resembling the rat but actually cousin to the hedgehog, was almost unknown in captivity, and the Adamses, having successfully risen to the challenge, presented their specimens to the grateful National and Bronx Zoos.)

Also with Frank, in 1913, Harriet made a six-month-long journey through the Far East that culminated on the Trans-Siberian Railway. From Hawaii they sailed to Japan and then on to the Philippines where they spent three months living among tribal peoples and speculating about the head-hunting proclivities of their new friends. They visited Borneo on the way to Singapore and eventually arrived in desolate Manchuria, via Hong Kong and Shanghai.

In the early 1920s, Harriet toured French and Spanish Morocco for a year with her sister, Anna, responding avidly to the desert environment. She was seduced especially by the mysteries of ancient Fez with its "walls within walls," "secluded gardens," and haunting "sound of running water." The sisters had arrived there in anecdote-rich discomfort, as passengers crowded into a friendly but breakdown-prone, long-distance jitney: The tickets for the journey had been purchased in a barber shop almost 300 miles away from the actual point of departure.

For Harriet, such colorful episodes were as bursts of wind to her sails, speeding her along even more pleasurably than usual. And since she had arranged her life always to be on the go, the only way to becalm her—war, after all, hadn't worked—seemed as if it would have to involve serious personal injury.

"You'll never walk again." This awful verdict was the one she heard from her doctors in 1927 when, in the Balearic Islands, she'd fallen off a cliff. Her back had been broken and she had been found by Spanish

*While visiting Paraguay, Harriet Chalmers Adams traded
a bottle of rum with a steamer captain for a squirming baby
grison (cousin to the polecat). Harriet traveled with her beloved
pet, whom she named Miss Bichy Mosqui, until the unfortunate
animal died after eating poisoned toucan stew in 1934.*

fishermen, who spotted her unable to move in the rising tide. A newspaper reported, "The medical care was better in intention than in scientific skill. No one knew how badly she was hurt, no one had an x-ray to find out."

Yet as it turned out, even this calamity was not enough to be a permanent setback to the 55-year-old world traveler, though she was forced to remain immobile for two years, strapped rigidly to a contrivance of board and restraints. During her convalescence, she remained as active as possible as the president of the Society of Women Geographers, a group she'd help organize two years earlier after becoming frustrated at the fact that women rarely gained full membership to other geographic societies.

Then, true to her promise, "I will travel again," Harriet resolutely put the status of invalid behind her in 1928, setting out alone that summer for seven months exploring Spain, Africa, and Asia Minor. Ignoring the almost constant pain she was still experiencing, she stoutly plunged on and, the following year, once more toured Spain and Portugal with Frank.

After Frank left for Washington, D.C., she continued on to fresh destinations. She traveled to Rumania, Turkey, Syria, and Libya, completing at last her long-cherished plan of visiting "every country in the old world or the new, in Europe, Asia, Africa and the islands of the seas" that had ever belonged to Spain or Portugal.

In her vibrant account for NATIONAL GEOGRAPHIC of her stay in "Cirenaica, Eastern Wing of Italian Libia" (June 1930), Harriet pronounced that region virtually *"terra incognita* to all save the heterogeneous peoples who for centuries have called it 'home,'" and, even more proudly, a place "where the tourist is not yet in evidence."

When Frank finally announced his retirement from the Pan American Union at the beginning of 1934, he and Harriet, planning, of course, to spend their time abroad, stored all of her travel journals, records, research, and photographs. (Tragically, a water leak later destroyed the entire archive beyond repair, leaving as testimony to her achievement only her published writings and six additional scrapbooks.)

During her last years, as she hopped from the Middle East to the British Isles, from the Balkans to the south of France, even the restless Harriet started to feel pangs of longing for the country of her birth or a settled residence. But Frank Adams' fears that the United States would prove too expensive for them overruled her yearnings. The couple continued traveling and Harriet once reassured a friend in a letter, "we are so rich in having one another."

Stricken suddenly with kidney disease, Harriet Chalmers Adams, like that other American globe-trotter, Fanny Bullock Workman, died on the French Riviera, having only recently arrived there from Athens. She was 62 years old when she at last went home to Stockton to be buried.

Harriet Chalmers Adams had crisscrossed the world, as she once said, "for the mere love of going." Early on she had intuited that the destiny that was hers to fulfill was to become that special creature—the "wandering lady." ■

"Think of what it is like

to stand at the edge of a cliff

surrounded by blue sky,

watching birds ride that ocean of air

with ease. Imagine...

wishing to lift off,

to skim over craggy peaks and

the tips of trees, then glide to

places beyond.

In the sea, this is what I do;

it is what anyone can do."

SYLVIA A. EARLE
1935 -

"AT FIRST I COULD SEE NOTHING but a taut white anchor line and murky green-gray water above and below as I descended hand over hand through increasing gloom. At 120 feet the view became strangely lighter, then white, like a snow-field extending in all directions.

"I suddenly realized what the snowfield was—squid eggs, millions of them. Abandoning the anchor line, I finned down into a bank of soft, cylindrical clusters of egg packets, each containing hundreds of developing young. I had landed in a marine nursery of colossal dimensions."

SPEND EVEN A LITTLE TIME with marine biologist and deep-sea explorer Sylvia Earle and the ocean will start to seem, as it does to her, like a permanent, liquid surprise party, continually churning up wriggling gifts and tentacled treats.

When she was a child, pond life thrilled her. Now, decades later, she's as excited by kelp as she ever was. Literally thousands of hours spent underwater haven't turned her soggy. And whether she's preaching her passionate doctrine of the centrality of ocean studies to the future of the planet or urging support for her crusade to encourage the establishment of more marine parks and sanctuaries, she possesses the remarkable gift of being able to make even seaweed seem sexy.

Dubbed "Her Royal Deepness" by colleagues, Sylvia has also heard herself called the U.S. "sturgeon general"—when she served as chief scientist of the National Oceanic and Atmospheric Administration from 1990 to 1992.

Since her first dive at the age of 17, into Florida's Weekiwachee River, wearing a borrowed helmet and meeting an alligator head on, she has earned her queenly status by going on to plunge to potentially lethal, record-breaking depths at sites around the world.

In 1970, with four other women ocean scientists, she spent two busy weeks living in an experimental underwater habitat. During that well-publicized stay ("Beacon Hill Housewife to Lead Team of Female Aquanauts" trumpeted the Boston Globe, referring to Dr. Earle, who at the time held fellowships at both Harvard and Radcliffe) she, with as much legitimacy as any passing fish, could claim a coral reef for her return address. (Even when selected as the National Geographic Society's explorer-in-residence in 1998, Sylvia Earle accepted the honor on the condition that she be allowed to list the sea as her official "residence.")

As for her friendly relations with some of the more than 25,000 species of fish—including sturgeon—with whom she has over the years cohabited, Sylvia Earle used to not rule out the possibility of enjoying a shore dinner now and then. Often asked whether she ever eats fish, her trenchant response would used to run along the lines of "Once in a while, but not anybody I know personally." Now she says, "I prefer seeing all sea creatures alive, swimming in the sea, rather than swimming in butter with lemon slices."

"WITHOUT SPECIAL EQUIPMENT, HUMAN BEINGS, like most other air-breathing creatures, cannot live underwater for long. With some practice, I can hold my breath for about a minute—time enough to swim around, touch bottom, 30 to 60 feet down, then race back to the surface, to sunlight, to air. Throughout history, humans have been divers in oceans worldwide, many going significantly deeper, and many staying much longer.

"However, it's important to remember," Sylvia Earle tells us, that, even when we are nowhere near it, "every breath we take is linked to the sea." Spurred on by her own understanding of this far-reaching truth, she has made it her special mission to promote greater recognition of the vital role oceans play when it comes to the health of the planet.

"There's plenty of water in the universe without life, but nowhere is there life without water.... *That's* why the ocean matters. If the sea is sick, we'll feel it. If it dies, we die. Our future and the state of the oceans are one."

Sometimes, she says, she has even tried to imagine what intelligent aliens, viewing it from afar, might think about Earth's topography. "From their perch in the sky, they could immediately see what many earthlings never seem to grasp: that this is a planet dominated by saltwater!"

Thus, for such a committed and indefatigable marine explorer as Sylvia Earle, one of the greatest unsolved mysteries of the sea is why her fellow humans appear so unresponsive to the crises of the world's oceans. To her it is incredible they can remain so unmoved by any sense of urgency to seek more knowledge about the oceans they sail on, fly over, eat fish from, and swim in. "Far and away the greatest threat to the sea and to the future of mankind is ignorance."

Emphasizing as she does the sea-linked origins of "every breath," her statement is obviously as much an individual, enacted truth as a higher, objective one. This, after all, is a woman who's lived underwater on nine different occasions.

"From the fishes' standpoint," she has written, "I was a noisy apparition of rushing bubbles, hose and huge helmet with legs, but I willed myself to be inconspicuous, and, as stealthily as I could, I made my way to them. Then, something unexpected happened. First one, then several and finally all of the small fish I had been stalking turned and swam in my direction. I was supposed to be the watcher but found myself the *watchee*, the center of attention for curious fish, apparently mesmerized by the strange bubbling being that had just fallen through their watery roof. For twenty blissful minutes, I became one with the river and its residents, bending with the current, blending in—and breathing!"

"LIKE MOST CHILDREN," SYLVIA RECALLS, "I was entranced by creepy crawly critters: horseshoe crabs, starfish, eels, blue crabs, sand flies, big jellyfish." And a story she frequently tells offers a snapshot of one early moment at the onset of her evolving marine obsession.

Born in 1935 and raised on a farm in New Jersey not far from the shore, she was a three-year-old playing on the beach one day when, suddenly, an Atlantic wave surged up and unexpectedly knocked her off her feet. "It tumbled me around in the surf, and at first I was panic stricken and overwhelmed. But after I caught my breath, I jumped back in."

One gives her credit, of course, for such precocious pluck in standing up to the ocean. But it was also as if, instinctively, she understood that the swirling water—this powerful and frightening, unknowable thing, with the largest possible aspects of it mysteriously hidden away—was only trying to get her attention.

As she grew older, she started to discover seagoing literature. Two books in particular increased her fascination with those secrets that awaited her beneath the waves. One of them, *Half Mile Down* by zoologist William Beebe, is an account of his then record-setting descent in 1934, 3,028 feet in a steel-hulled submersible, the *Bathysphere*. The other, *On the Bottom* (1929), was by a U.S. Navy commander, Edward Ellsberg, and thrilled her with its stories of deep-sea salvage operations.

As a result, when in 1948 her family moved to Dunedin, a small town near Tampa Bay, on Florida's west coast, Sylvia was ecstatic to find the Gulf of Mexico was now her backyard and stood ready to take every advantage from the fact.

However, it required only her first actual dive, a

friend's father's copper diving helmet heavy on her bare shoulders, for her to understand that the fear that had seasoned her anticipation was measurably real. Entranced by everything she was seeing (and that was watching her back) through the clear water of the river bottom, she realized—almost too late—that her dizziness had to be the result of something more than the intense excitement of the long-awaited moment. Pulled to the surface with a mixture of toxic gases seeping into her oxygen supply, she learned her first important lesson—never, ever, take clean air for granted.

Fortunately, that same year, 1952, Sylvia eagerly read in Jacques-Yves Cousteau's book, *The Silent World*, that this Frenchman had recently invented a less cumbersome "scuba" apparatus aimed at facilitating undersea observation. At Florida State University's Alligator Harbor Marine Laboratory, the 18-year-old student Sylvia soon was donning the local equipment, determined to master it. It was 1953 and the "urge to submerge" she was indulging was about to turn into the guiding impulse behind a life's work.

BY 1969, EARLE HAD BEEN MARRIED TWICE and was raising three children. She also was a seasoned veteran of what she calls the "lovely, living saltwater soup." Specializing in the biology of algae, she had been awarded her doctorate from Duke University three years earlier after completing her dissertation, "Phaeophyta of the Eastern Gulf of Mexico."

It was at the instigation of her second husband, Giles Mead, then curator of fishes at Harvard's Museum of Comparative Zoology, that she stopped to check out an announcement on the bulletin board there about Phase II of Project Tektite. The project, a saturation diving study sponsored by the U.S. Navy in conjunction with NASA, the Department of the Interior, and other agencies, was seeking applicants to conduct independent research projects in the summer of 1970. If accepted, she could expect something she had only dreamed of—an underwater habitat that obviated the need for the stopwatch expeditions to which she was accustomed and offered a constantly "open" doorway straight into the sea.

"Two weeks! Not just in and out for half an hour or so at a time, three or four times a day, but all day, every day, and all night. Underwater for 14 days straight! What a concept!" she thought to herself.

The only thing Sylvia hadn't counted on was the idea that a coed environment might be considered unsuitable even for qualified scientists. She would wind up joining an all women aquanaut team as a way of assuring propriety; the other four members, like herself, were serious students of the marine environment.

During moonlit underwater swims, Earle and her colleagues were thrilled to observe blue chromis damselfish differentiate real enemies from dummy ones, or to see parrotfish sleep suspended in the viscous cocoons they spin around themselves. In fact, the coral reef resembled nothing so much as a quick-stop, low-rent motel, with new guests checking into their niches before the linens, so to speak, had even been freshened from the last visitor. Sylvia Earle termed it "hot bunking," and it did make for entertaining, piscatorial voyeurism. "Stay underwater long enough," she says, "and individual fish become recognizable…as very specific characters whose habits become as familiar as those of neighbors…."

The Tektite laboratory, submerged at 50 feet, was

attached by cable hookups to the shore, 600 feet away. Inside its snug but well-equipped quarters (taped music and Stouffer's frozen meals were among the amenities), the women themselves were under 24-hour recorded surveillance, as much a part of the ongoing Tektite experiment as any damselfish.

When the moment came, regretfully, to depart, Sylvia and the other aquanauts were required first to swim into a nearby open diving bell, which next was sealed off before allowing them to transfer into a surface chamber of equal pressurization. They then had to endure this decompression period for almost an entire day.

"It did not seem a bad trade-off: 21 hours parked in a metal cylinder decompressing in order to have 336 hours of continuous underwater time. I had traveled much longer crunched into the confines of other metal cylinders—airplanes—to have far fewer hours of diving on distant reefs."

NEARLY A DECADE LATER, SYLVIA EARLE would settle for two and a half hours in the waters off Oahu, in the Hawaiian Islands—but she would not be exploring at 50 feet, or even 100 feet (the maximum depth of excursions made from Tektite) beneath the Pacific surface. Rather, on this record-shattering dive, covered by a futuristically bizarre-looking "Jim suit" (named after Jim Jarratt, its first wearer) and tethered to a manned submersible, she would be walking 1,250 feet under the sea, with the water pressure outside of Jim at 600 pounds per square inch.

"Sylvia really does have nerves of steel," her longtime underwater partner, photographer Al Giddings once told a journalist. Even he, frequent witness to many of what he calls Sylvia's "very hairy diving expeditions" (involving

Sylvia Earle captures a sea snake in Australian waters.
Sea snakes are highly poisonous, and,
unlike land snakes, few antivenins have been developed
to counteract the harmful effects of its venom.

sharks and long-term exposure to the ocean's depths,) felt twinges of uncharacteristic apprehensive anxiety before setting off alongside her in the submersible from which she would emerge. Here's how Sylvia recounted those first moments at maximum depth:

"'Five hundred feet, still descending,' Al's voice fills the dome surrounding my head. 'How are you feeling?'"

"I want to answer, 'Extraordinary! Fantastic!' But I respond with the dignity appropriate to a scientific experiment: 'Fine, no problems,' and the descent continues."

SYLVIA'S WAS THE FIRST OPEN-OCEAN USE of the 1,200 pound Jim; previously always tethered to the surface, it had been employed in submarine salvage and offshore oil operations. However, to her, the two-and-a-half hours she spent roaming inside it seemed more like a mere 20 minutes.

Whether communing with equally well-armored crabs ("I think I know how you feel," she quipped silently to one as it crossed her path) or admiring the luminescent blue flashes given off by the spiral stalks of bamboo coral, she was oblivious to anything but the visual spectacles and pioneer joys she was experiencing. And she was continually aware that the place she was enjoying them in was as remote to the rest of her own species as any distant galaxy.

Planting an American flag on the seafloor, she also returned to the surface with a specimen stick of the bamboo coral *(Lepidisis olapa)* that she presented to the National Geographic Society. (It is now on view in a tailored glass case in the Society's library.) Seven years later, in 1986, as a very different sort of souvenir of her fearless Jim-testing expedition, she married the suit's English designer, Graham Hawkes. With him, she had already founded Deep Ocean

Engineering, a company devoted to building such innovative, easy-to-handle underwater vessels as *Deep Rover, Phantom*, and, later, *Deep Flight*.

Though she separated from Hawkes in 1990, Earle—whom Al Giddings once described as "moving at Mach 10"—is hardly persuasive when she claims she's no "superwoman or superperson." In 1992 she founded a new company, Deep Ocean Exploration and Research, for scientific consulting and management of marine operations.

Since childhood "a vision of wanting to understand life in the ocean" helped drive her on. But it was equally important that she also understood that her temperament demanded "true exploration," rather than indulging in a kind of scientific guessing game based on those "things washed up on the beach." Moreover, despite her countless entrances and exits from an often cold and dark, invariably damp and inevitably unpredictable environment where dwell "organisms that might regard us as simply another meal," the idea of her own courage has never entered into it. Insists Earle, "I'm more frightened every day when I get on the highway."

Often movingly eloquent in her musings, Sylvia Earle is able to infuse even statistical information with the spirit of poetry. For her, every underwater hour heightens "the excitement of the last as one discovery leads to another [and] each new scrap of information trigger[s] awareness of dozens of new unknowns."

"What we've physically seen of the ocean world is equal to about what lies inside the city limits of Baltimore," she points out, then adds dryly, "Never mind that you have to start at the top and work down." ■

AFTERWORD

Susan Fifer Canby
Director, Libraries & Indexing
NATIONAL GEOGRAPHIC SOCIETY

CAN A LIBRARIAN CONFINED BY her silent, book-lined walls make a discovery about—of all things—the exotic field of exploration and discovery? She can if the walls are those of the National Geographic Society and if the books that line them include the journals, letters, and images of classic and contemporary explorers, whose derring-do has often been overlooked because they were women.

These books are the origin and heart of *Living with Cannibals and Other Women's Adventures*. They were written by some of the world's boldest adventurers, by women who overcame not only peril and privation in remote lands, but also the restraints of society that often looked askance at such unorthodox behavior.

I came across this rich subject almost accidentally, while working in the collections of the Society's fine library that I have managed for more than 25 years. Filed among the well-known works of Peary, Byrd, and other male explorers, I found writings by women largely unknown to the public, but no less exciting.

Obviously these wonderful accounts, along with many more, were material for a book, already long overdue. I found myself wondering what motivated these women to forsake the comfort and security of home and undertake long, arduous, and often perilous journeys. I reflected on the way the early women travelers helped set the stage for modern-day women adventurers. I was also glad to see that often a link existed between the National Geographic and adventuring women throughout the Society's more than 110-year history.

Certainly, travel to distant lands offered adventure and freedoms unthinkable at home. Often these women seemed prompted by a desire to escape gender restrictions, or more personal constraints such as grief or family responsibilities. While male explorers traditionally enjoyed the sponsorship of governments or learned societies, women seemed to travel less burdened by expectations. They were free to interact with other cultures, particularly other women, in a way that men could not. The fact that the women explorers themselves were considered harmless, or a curiosity, facilitated dialogue and often opened doors to the more private, or everyday, aspects of the people whose lives they shared as they traveled from country to country.

Regardless, the women traveled forth. Over time, they added to geographic knowledge, carried new ideas to the rest of the world, and, by winning acceptance as women in traditionally male roles, contributed to the emancipation of women. So doing, they laid the groundwork for contemporary adventurers, many with whom the Society has collaborated and whose stories are in this book.

The National Geographic Society welcomes these contemporary women as part of its special travel and adventure collection, while commemorating the ladies of the past who paved the way.

The bibliography that follows offers a few of the first person narratives about women explorers found in the Society's library. ■

BIBLIOGRAPHY

Adams, Harriet Chalmers.
NATIONAL GEOGRAPHIC: European
  Outpost: The Azores. 35-66, *Jan.*
  1935; Madeira the Florescent. 81-
  106, *July 1934;* River-Encircled
  Paraguay. 385-416, *Apr. 1933;*
  Madrid Out-of-Doors. 225-256,
  Aug 1931; Cirenaica, Eastern
  Wing of Italian Libya. 689-726,
  June 1930; Barcelona, Pride of the
  Catalans. 373-402, *Mar. 1929;*
  An Altitudinal Journey Through
  Portugal. 567-610, *Nov 1927;*
  Across French and Spanish
  Morocco. 327-356, *Mar. 1925;*
  Volcano-Girded Salvador.
  189-200, *Feb. 1922;* The Grand
  Canyon Bridge. 645-650, *June
  1921;* Rio de Janeiro, in the Land
  of Lure. 165-210, *Sept. 1920;* In
  French Lorraine. 499-518, *Nov-
  Dec 1917;* The First Transandine
  Railroad from Buenos Aires to
  Valparaiso. 397-417, *May 1910;*
  Kaleidoscopic La Paz: The City
  of the Clouds. 119-141, *Feb, 1909;*
  Cuzco, America's Ancient
  Mecca. 669-689, *Oct. 1908;* Some
  Wonderful Sights in the Andean
  Highlands. 597-618, *Sept. 1908;*
  Along the Old Inca Highway
  (Peru). 231-250, *Apr. 1908*; The
  East Indians in the New World
  (Trinidad). 485-491, *July 1907.*

Bancroft, Anne.
Religions of the East. New York:
  St. Martin's Press, 1974.
Women in the Antarctic. New York:
  Harrington Park Press, 1988.

Bates, Daisy.
*The Passing of the Aborigines:
  A Lifetime Spent Among Natives of
  Australia.* London: J. Murray, 1966.

Beckwith, Carol.
African Ceremonies. New York:
  Harry N. Abrams, 1999.
*African Ark: the People and Ancient
  Cultures of Ethiopia and the Horn
  of Africa.* New York: Harry N.
  Abrams, 1990.
Nomads of Niger. New York:
  H. N. Abrams, 1983.
  –NATIONAL GEOGRAPHIC: African
  Marriage Rituals. 80-97, *Nov.
  1999;* Masai Passage to Manhood.
  52-65, *Sept. 1999;* Brides of the
  Sahara. 80-91, *Feb. 1998;* Royal
  Gold of the Asante Empire.
  36-47, *Oct. 1996;* African Roots
  of Voodoo. 102-113, *Aug. 1995;*
  Fantasy Coffins of Ghana. 120-
  130, *Sept. 1994;* Eloquent Surma
  of Ethiopia. 77-99, *Feb. 1991;*
  Niger's Wodaabe: "People of the
  Taboo." 483-509, *Oct. 1983.*

Bell, Gertrude Lowthian.
The Letters of Gertrude Bell.
  London: E. Benn, 1927.
Syria: The Desert & the Sown.
  New York: E.P. Dutton, 1907.

Bird, Isabella Lucy (Bishop).
*Account of the Vicissitudes and
  Position of the Country.* London:
  J. Murray, 1905.
*A Lady's Life in the Rocky
  Mountains.* Norman: University
  of Oklahoma Press, 1960.
  (Originally published 1879.)
*Unbeaten Tracks in Japan: An
  Account of Travels in the Interior
  Including Visits to the Aborigines of
  Yezo and the Shrines of Nikko and
  Ise.* London: J. Murray, 1880.
*The Yangtze Valley and Beyond: An
  Account of Journeys in China, Chiefly
  in the Province of Sze Chuan and
  Among the Man -Tze of the Somo
  Territory.* London: J. Murray, 1900.

Boyd, Louise Arner.
*The Coast of Northeast Greenland,
  with Hydrographic Studies in the
  Greenland Sea. The Louise A. Boyd
  Arctic Expeditions of 1937 and
  1938.* New York: American
  Geographical Society, 1948.
The Fiord Region of East Greenland.

New York: American Geographical Society, 1939.

Polish Countrysides. New York: American Geographical Society, 1937.

Blum, Arlene.
Annapurna, a Woman's Place. San Francisco: Sierra Club Books, 1980.

Cable Mildred, & Francesca French.
The Gobi Desert. London: Hodder and Stoughton, 1942.
Through Jade Gate and Central Asia: An Account of Journeys in Kansu, Turkestan and the Gobi Desert. London: Constable, 1927.

Cameron, Agnes Deans.
The New North: Being Some Account of a Woman's Journey through Canada to the Arctic. New York: D. Appleton, 1910.

Chapman, Olive Murray.
Across Lapland with Sledge and Reindeer. New York: Dodd, 1930.
Across Iceland, the Land of Frost and Fire. New York: Dodd, 1930.

Cheesman, Evelyn.
Camping Adventures on Cannibal Islands. London: Harrap, 1949.
Islands Near the Sun; Off the Beaten Path in the Far, Fair Society Islands. London: H.F. & G. Witherby, 1927.

Clark, Eugenie.
The Fishes of the Red Sea: Order Plectognathi. Cairo: Fouad University Press, 1953.
Shark Lady: True Adventures of Eugenie Clark. New York: Four Winds Press, 1978.
NATIONAL GEOGRAPHIC: Whale Sharks, Gentle Monsters of the Deep. 125-139, *Dec.1992;* Surugu Bay: In the Shadow of Mount Fuji. 2-39, *Oct. 1990;* Down the Cayman Wall. 712-731, *Nov. 1988;* Sharks at 2,000 Feet. 681-691, *Nov. 1986*; Japan's Izu

Oceanic Park. 465-491, *Apr. 1984*; Hidden Life of an Undersea Desert. 129-144, *July 1983;* Sharks: Magnificent and Misunderstood. 138-187, *Aug. 1981*; Flashlight Fish of the Red Sea. 719-728, *Nov 1978*; Into the Lairs of "Sleeping" Sharks. 570-584, *Apr. 1975;* The Red Sea's Sharkproof Fish. 718-727, *Nov. 1974;* The Red Sea's Garden of Eels. 724-735, *Nov 1972.*

David-Neel, Alexandra.
Magic and Mystery in Tibet. New York: C. Kendall, 1932.
My Journey to Lhasa: The Personal Story of the Only White Woman Who Succeeded in Entering the Forbidden City. New York: Harper, 1927.

Davidson, Robyn.
Desert Places. New York: Viking, 1996.
From Alice to Ocean : Alone Across the Outback. Reading, MA: Addison Wesley, 1992.
Tracks. London: J.Cape, 1980.
NATIONAL GEOGRAPHIC: Wandering with India's Rabiri. 64-93, *Sep. 1993;* Alone Across the Outback. 581-611, *May 1978.*

Denker, Debra.
Sisters on the Bridge of Fire: Journeys in the Crucible of High Asia. Los Angeles : Burning Gate Press, 1993.
NATIONAL GEOGRAPHIC: Along Afghanistan's War-torn Frontier. 772-797, *June 1985;* Pakistan's Kalash: People of Fire and Fervour. 458-473, *Oct. 1981.*

Earhart, Amelia.
The Fun of it; Random Records of my own Flying and of Women in Aviation. New York: Brewer, Warren & Putnam, 1932.
Last Flight. New York: Harcourt, Brace, 1937.
20 Hrs. 40 Min.; Our Flight in the Friendship. The American Girl,

First Across the Atlantic by Air; Tells Her Story. New York, London: G.P. Putnam's Sons, 1928.
NATIONAL GEOGRAPHIC: Amelia Earhart. 112-135, *Jan 1998;* My Flight from Hawaii. 593-609, *May 1935.*

Earle, Sylvia A.
Sea Change: A Message of the Oceans. New York: Putnam's Sons, 1995.
Earle, Sylvia A. and Al Giddings. *Exploring the Deep Frontier: The Adventure of Man in the Sea*. Washington: National Geographic Society, 1980.
Earle, Sylvia and Henry Wolcott. *Wild Ocean: America's Parks Under the Sea*. Washington: National Geographic Society, 1999.
NATIONAL GEOGRAPHIC: Persian Gulf Pollution. 122-134, *Feb.1992;* Undersea World of a Kelp Forest. 411-426, *Sept. 1980;* A Walk in the Deep. 624-631, *May 1980;* Humpbacks: The Gentle Giants. 2-17, *Jan. 1979;* Life Springs from Death in Truk Lagoon. 578-603, *May 1976;* All-girl Team Tests the Habitat. 291-296, *Aug. 1971.*

Forbes, Rosita Torr.
India of the Princes. New York: E. P. Dutton, Inc., 1941.
The Secret of the Sahara: Kufara. New York: George H. Doran, 1921.
The Sultan of the Mountains: The Life Story of Raisuli. New York: H. Holt, 1924.
Adventure: Being a Gipsy Salad... New York: Houghton Mifflin, 1928.
Islands in the Sun. London, Evans Bros., 1950.

Fossey, Dian.
The Behaviour of the Mountain Gorilla. Thesis – Darwin College, 1976.
Gorillas in the Mist. Boston: Houghton Mifflin, 1983.

Galdikas, Biruté M. F.
Orangutan Odyssey. New York: Harry N. Abrams, 1999.
Reflections of Eden: My Years with the Orangutans of Borneo. Boston: Little Brown, 1995.
NATIONAL GEOGRAPHIC:Living with the Great Orange Apes: Indonesia's Orangutans. 830-853, *June 1980;* Orangutans, Indonesia's "People of the Forest." 444-473, *Oct. 1975*

Goodall, Jane.
My Friends, the Wild Chimpanzees. Washington D.C.: National Geographic Society, 1967.
Behaviour of Free-living Chimpanzees in the Gombe Stream Reserve. London: Balliere, Tindall and Cassell, 1968.
Grub the Bush Baby. London: Collins, 1970.
Chimpanzees of Gombe : Patterns of Behaviour. Cambridge, Mass.: Belknap Press of Harvard University Press, 1986.
My Life with the Chimpanzees. New York: Pocket Books, 1988.
The Chimpanzee Family Book. Saxonville, MA: Picture Book Studio, 1989.
In the Shadow of Man. Boston: Houghton Mifflin, 1988.
Through a Window : My Thirty Years with the Chimpanzees of Gombe. Boston: Houghton Mifflin, 1990.
Reason for Hope : A Spiritual Journey. New York: Warner Books, 1999.
NATIONAL GEOGRAPHIC: Crusading for Chimps and Humans. 102-129, *Dec. 1995;* Life and Death at Gombe. 592-621, *May 1979;* Tool-using Bird; The Egyptian Vulture. 631-641, *May 1968;* New Discoveries Among Africa's Chimpanzees. 802-831, *Dec. 1965;* My Life Among Wild Chimpanzees. 272-308, *Aug. 1963.*

Kingsley, Mary Henrietta.
Travels in West Africa: Congo Francais, Corisco and Cameroons. London: F.Cass, 1965.

Leakey, Mary D.
Excavations at the Njoro River Cave: Stone Age Cremated Burials in Kenya Colony. Oxford: Clarendon Press, 1950.
Olduvai Gorge : My Search for Early Man. London: Collins, 1979.
Africa's Vanishing Art : The Rock Paintings of Tanzania. Garden City, New York: Doubleday, 1983.
Disclosing the Past. Garden City, New York: Doubleday, 1984.
NATIONAL GEOGRAPHIC: Tanzania's Stone Age Art. 84-99, *July 1983;* Footprints in the Ashes of Time. 446-457, *Apr. 1979.*

Lindbergh, Anne Morrow.
Gift from the Sea. New York: Vintage Books, 1978.
Dearly Beloved; a Theme and Variations. New York, Harcourt, Brace & World, 1962.
Listen! the Wind. New York: Harcourt, Brace and Company, 1938.
North to the Orient. New York: Harcourt, Brace and Company, 1935.
NATIONAL GEOGRAPHIC: Flying Around the North Atlantic. 259-337, *Sept. 1934.*

Marsden, Kate.
On Sledge and Horseback to Outcast Siberian Lepers. New York: Cassell, 1892.

Mead, Margaret.
Aspects of the Present. New York: Morrow, 1980.
Letters from the Field, 1925-1975. New York: Harper & Row, 1979.
Anthropologists and What They Do. New York: F.Watts, 1965.
Coming of Age in Samoa. New York: Morrow, 1961.
Mountain Arapesh. New York: American Museum
of Natural History, 1938.

Momatiuk, Yva.
This Marvelous Terrible Place: Images of Newfoundland and Labrador. Camden East, Ontario: Firefly Books, 1998.
High Country. Sydney: Reed, 1980.
NATIONAL GEOGRAPHIC: Slovakia's Spirit of Survival. 120-146, *Jan. 1987;* Maoris: At Home in Two Worlds. 522-541, *Oct. 1984;* Poland's Mountain People. 104-129, *Jan. 1981;* New Zealand's High Country. 246-265, *Aug. 1978;* Still Eskimo, Still Free: The Inuit of Umingmatok. 624-647, *Nov. 1977.*

Murphy, Dervla.
Muddling Through in Madagascar. London: J. Murray, 1985.
Cameroon with Egbert. London: J. Murray, 1989.
Eight Feet in the Andes. London: J. Murray, 1983.
In Ethiopia with a Mule. London: J. Murray, 1968.
Ireland. Salem: Salem House, 1985.
A Place Apart. Old Greenwich: Devin-Adir, 1978.
The Waiting Land: A Spell in Nepal. London: J. Murray, 1967.
Where the Indus is Young: A Winter in Baltistan. London: J. Murray, 1977.

Peary, Josephine Diebitsch.
My Arctic Journal: A Year Among the Ice-Fields and Eskimos. New York: Contemporary Publishing, 1893.
The Snow Baby: A True Story with True Pictures. New York: F.A. Stokes Company, 1901.
Children of the Arctic. New York: F.A. Stokes Company, 1903.

Peck, Annie Smith.
A Search for the Apex of America: High Mountain Climbing in Peru and Bolivia, Including the Conquest of Huascaran, with Some Observations on the Country and People Below.

New York: Dodd, Mead, 1911

Pfeiffer, Ida.
A Lady's Voyage Round the World: a Selected Translation from the German of Ida Pfeiffer. London: Century, 1988. (Originally published 1850.)
A Journey to Iceland and Travels in Sweden and Norway. New York: G. P. Putnam, 1852.

Ride, Sally.
Voyager : an Adventure to the Edge of the Solar System. New York: Crown Publishers, 1992.
To Space & Back. New York: Lothrop, Lee & Shepard, 1986.

Rijnhart, Susie Carson.
With the Tibetans in Tent and Temple; Narrative of Four Years' Residence on the Tibetan Border, and of a Journey into the Far Interior. Chicago: Fleming H. Revell, 1904.

Scidmore, Eliza Ruhamah.
Alaska, its Southern Coast and the Sitkan Archipelago. Boston: D. Lothrop & Co., 1885.
Jinrikisha Days in Japan. New York: Harper & Bros, 1891.
China, the Long-lived empire. New York: The Century Co., 1900.
Java, the Garden of the East. New York: The Century Co., 1907.
NATIONAL GEOGRAPHIC: Adam's Secret Eden. 105-173, 206, *Feb. 1912;* Mukden, the Manchu Home and its Great Art Museum. 289-320, *Apr. 1910;* Koyasan, the Japanese Valhalla, 650-670, *Oct. 1907;* Archaeology in the Air. 151-163, *Mar. 1907;* Bathing and Burning Ghats at Benares. 118-128, *Feb. 1907;* The Greatest Hunt in the World. 673-692, *Dec 1906;* Mrs. Bishop's "The Yangtze Valley and Beyond." 366-368, *Sept. 1900;* The Tsung-Li-Yamen. 291-292, *July 1900;* Sitkine River in 1898. 1-15,

Jan. 1899; The Mt. St. Elias Expedition of Prince Luigi Amadeo of Savoy. 1897. 93-96, *Mar. 1898;* The Recent Earthquake Wave on the Coast of Japan. 285-289, *Sept. 1896.* Recent Explorations in Alaska. 173-179, *Jan. 1894.*

Stark, Freya Madaline.
The Arab Island, the Middle East, 1939-1943. New York: Knopf, 1945.
Baghdad Sketches. New York: Dutton, 1939.
Seen in the Hadhramat. New York: Dutton, 1939.
The Southern Gates of Arabia; A Journey in the Hadhramat. New York: Dutton, 1936.
The Valley of the Assassins and Other Persian Travels. London: J. Murray, 1934.
A Winter in Arabia. London: J. Murray, 1940.

Thayer, Helen.
Polar Dream. New York: Delta, 1995.

Workman, Fanny Bullock.
Peaks and Glaciers of Nun Kun; A Record of Pioneer-Exploration and Mountaineering in the Punjab Himalaya. London: Constable and Company Ltd., 1909.
Two Summers in the Ice-Wilds of Eastern Karakoram; the Exploration of Nineteen Hundred Square Miles of Mountain and Glacier. New York: E.P. Dutton & Company, 1917
Workman, Fanny Bullock and William Hunter Workman. *In the World of Himalaya, Among the Peaks and Passes of Ladakh, Nubra, Suru, and Baltistan.* New York: Cassell & Company Ltd. 1900.

Yeager, Jeana.
Voyager. New York: Knopf : Distributed by Random House, 1987.

WOMEN WHO
PUSHED THE LIMITS
HIGHLIGHTS FROM HISTORY

■ A.D. 381—ETHERIA, a nun, travels to Jerusalem and Egypt, and writes a guide to the Holy Land for pilgrims.

■ A.D. 700 — After a nun teaches her to use a sword, NIEH YIN-NIANG travels through the Chinese countryside avenging the poor and downtrodden.

■ A.D. 1000 —Legendary Viking AUD THE DEEP MINDED, sails from Norway to Scotland and then to Iceland, claiming land that she later grants to her children and followers.

■ 1390—In the book *Canterbury Tales* by Geoffrey Chaucer, pilgrims tells stories to help pass the time as they journey to the shrine of Thomas Becket. One pilgrim, THE WIFE OF BATH, says, "If wommen hadde writen stories.... They wolde han writen of men more wikkednesse/Than all the mark of Adam may redresse."

■ 1492—QUEEN ISABELLA of Spain sponsors the voyage of explorer Christopher Columbus. When her troops went to battle, she was known to join them.

■ 1700s—Pirate ANNE BONNY is joined in high seas adventures by her female cohort MARY READ. It is said that when the lady pirate's ship was boarded and most of the crew fled below deck for safety, Anne taunted them saying, "Dogs! instead of these weaklings, if I only had some women with me!"

■ 1704—SARAH KEMBLE KNIGHT travels alone by horseback from Boston to New Haven, then publishes an account of the adventure entitled *Madame Knight*.

■ 1716—LADY MARY WORTLEY MONTAGU scandalizes London by traveling without her husband to Constantinople. She enjoys the excursion so much that she spends the rest of her life traveling throughout the Middle East, often dressed in native garb.

■ 1784—ELIZABETH THIBLE of Lyons, France, becomes the first woman to soar in a hot air balloon.

■ 1804—A Lemhi Shoshoni girl, SACAJEWEA, joins the Lewis and Clark expedition as translator and ambassador to some of the Native American territories that the party will cross. Captain Lewis writes in his journal of Sacajewea after a pirogue nearly sinks,

"Sacajawea demonstrates fortitude and resolution equal to that of any man on board the stricken craft. She saved most of the bundles which had been washed overboard."

■ 1837—LADY JANE FRANKLIN becomes the first woman to summit Mount Wellington in New Zealand—a near vertical climb of 4,000 feet.

■ 1846—IDA PFEIFFER embarks on her first of three voyages around the world. During her second voyage, she lives among cannibals and headhunters on Borneo and Sumatra.

■ 1858—JULIA ARCHIBALD HOLMES climbs Colorado's Pikes Peak "I have accomplished the task which I marked out for myself.... Nearly everyone tried to discourage me from attempting it, but I believed that I should succeed," she writes.

■ 1863—ELIZABETH L. VAN LEW travels the southern United States in the capacity of a spy for the Union military.

■ 1864—FLORENCE BAKER and husband Samuel explore Lake Albert, an important source of the Nile. Samuel is awarded the Royal Geographical Society's gold medal and later knighted for his efforts; but Queen Victoria, scandalized by Florence's past, refuses to receive her at court.

■ 1864—ANNA LEONOWENS travels from her home in London to Singapore, then to Siam to give a European education to the 67 children of King Rama IV. The story will later be chronicled in Margaret Landon's book, *Anna and the King of Siam*, which was based on Leonowen's journal.

■ 1873—ISABELLA BIRD BISHOP fulfills her dreams of travel as she sets out for Hawaii from Edinburgh, Scotland via Australia. She then travels to the U.S.

■ 1878—AMANDA BERRY SMITH embarks on a 12-year missionary journey, which includes 8 years spent in Liberia. She spends the rest of her travels on three different continents. Born as slave in Maryland in 1837, Smith gained her freedom and emerged as one of the 19th century's most important Christian evangelists.

■ 1889—Inspired by the fictional character appearing in the novel *Around the World in 80 Days* by Jules Verne, NELLIE BLY races around the world in 72 days, 6 hours, and 11 minutes. She says, "The trip to Amiens was slow and tiresome, but I was fully repaid for the journey by meeting Jules Verne and his wife, who were waiting for me at the station in company with the *World's* Paris correspondent."

■ 1890s—MARY BIRD travels 500 miles alone, by camel, to reach Persia, where she was sent by the Christian Missionary Society to start a mission.

■ 1891—ZOE GAYTON wins a $2,000 wager after walking across the United States. The trip took 213 days.

■ 1891—MARY FRENCH SHELDON travels to East Africa making groundbreaking anthropological discoveries. Later, the Royal Geographical Society revokes her membership because of debate over women's presence in the organization.

■ 1892—KATE MARSDEN publishes *On Sledge and Horseback to Outcast Siberian Lepers*, an account of her journeys across Siberia to help find a cure for leprosy.

■ 1893—MARY KINGSLEY begins zoological research in West Africa. She returns two years later to pioneer a route through the Gabon, and ascends Mount Cameroon. Even on rough terrain she kept an analytical mind: "One appalling corner I shall not forget, for I had to jump at a rock wall and hang on to it in a manner more befitting an insect than an insect-hunter, and then scramble up into a close-set forest, heavily burdened with boulders of all sizes. I wonder whether the rocks or the trees came first?"

■ 1893—TESSIE REYNONDS, at the age of 16, rides a bicycle roundtrip from Brighton to London, England. Her long jacket over knickers outrages the public as much as her feat.

■ 1895—ANNIE OAKLEY breaks tradition by wearing shorter dresses and carrying a rifle during the height of the Victorian era. Her sharpshooting skills earn her the name "Little Sure Shot" and allow her to travel throughout North America and Europe.

■ 1899—GERTRUDE BELL makes her first of several desert journeys. She goes to Jebel Druze, becoming the first European woman to travel in remote parts of the Middle East.

■ 1901—ANNIE TAYLOR becomes the first person to plunge over Niagara Falls in a custom-built barrel and live. She took on the challenge even though she couldn't swim. Her comment on being retrieved: "Nobody ever ought to do that again."

■ 1906—FANNY BULLOCK WORKMAN breaks the woman's altitude record by reaching 23,300 feet on Nun Kun peak in what is now India.

■ 1908—ANNIE SMITH PECK, the first woman to reach the Matterhorn's peak, claims to break Fanny Bullock Workman's climbing record. "If you are determined to commit suicide, why don't you do it in a lady-like manner?" writes her father in a letter to Annie.

■ 1910—CLELIA DUEL MOSHER shatters popular myths about female health, including one claiming women breathe differently than men, which makes them unfit for strenuous exercise.

■ 1910—BLANCHE STUART SCOTT, 19, becomes the first woman to fly a plane solo. Earlier the same year she completes a cross-country trip in an Overland automobile with a woman journalist along to record the trip.

■ 1910—NAN JANE ASPINALL leaves San Francisco on horseback to make a solo journey across the United States. Her final destination is New York.

■ 1912—Navigating through dense fog, HARRIET QUIMBY becomes the first woman to pilot an airplane across the English Channel.

■ 1914—NATIONAL GEOGRAPHIC publishes some of its first color photographs which were hand tinted by geographer and associate editor ELIZA R. SCIDMORE. Scidmore spent years as a roving reporter for the Society, traveling around the world on ventures that saw her on a royal elephant hunt with the King of Siam to visiting "where the butterflies danced" in what is now Sri Lanka.

■ 1916—HARRIET CHALMERS ADAMS is the first woman correspondent to report on World War I from the front lines.

■ 1916—Sisters ADELINE and AUGUSTA VAN BUREN ride motorcycles across the United States. They leave Brooklyn on July 5 and arrive in San Francisco on September 12. Afterward, the team rides their motorcycles up Pikes Peak in Colorado.

■ 1916—By installing auxiliary gas tanks, upping her fuel capacity from 8 to 53 gallons, and adding a rubber gas line to her open "pusher" type Curtiss plane, RUTH LAW flies nonstop from Chicago to Hornell, New York, setting the American nonstop cross-country record for both men and women.

■ 1920—MARGARET MEAD begins a life of anthropological studies, as she travels to New Guinea and the Pacific Islands. "The natives are superficially agreeable," she writes home, "but they go in for cannibalism, headhunting, infanticide, incest, avoidance and joking relationships, and biting lice in half with their teeth."

■ 1924—ALEXANDRA DAVID-NEEL enters Tibet. She faces great adversity, but finally reaches the forbidden lands of Lhasa. She comments, "If Heaven is the Lord's, the earth is the inheritance of Man...consequently, any honest traveller has the right to walk as he chooses, all over the globe which is his."

■ 1926—BESSIE COLEMAN dies in a plane crash in Jacksonville, Florida, after performing at air shows from coast to coast. As the first black woman to receive her pilot's license in 1921, she said, "The air is the only place free from prejudices."

■ 1926—After successfully becoming the sixth person to swim the English Channel from France to England, GERTRUDE EDERLE joins the vaudeville circuit, traveling with a collapsible swimming pool. By 1933, she had become deaf, and takes on a new career teaching deaf children to swim.

■ 1928—ROSITA FORBES publishes her account of "twelve highly seasoned years," in Arabia and North Africa where she spent time living in a harem, witnessing "black magic," and going on a pilgrimage to Mecca.

■ 1930—AMY JOHNSON sets a speed record of 13 days flying from London to India, then on to Australia. She becomes popularly known as the "Darling of the Sky."

■ 1931—GLORIA HOLLISTER ANABLE descends 1,208 feet below the surface of the ocean in a bathysphere, setting a new women's diving record.

■ 1931—LOUISE ARNER BOYD organizes the first of four expeditions to East Greenland. Twenty-four years later, she becomes the first woman to reach the North Pole.

■ 1932—AMELIA EARHART flies solo across the Atlantic. On July 2, 1937, she disappears after completing 22,000 of the 29,000 miles it takes to fly around the world at the Equator, the longest way possible.

■ 1932—In April, FLORENCE CLASR summits, via dogsled team, New Hampshire's Mount Washington.

■ 1934—JEANETTE PICCARD pilots a 175-foot zeppelin 57,559 feet into the stratosphere.

■ 1934—ANNE MORROW LINDBERGH receives the National Geographic Society Hubbard Medal—awarded for distinction in exploration, discovery, and research—for "Notable flights, as copilot, on Charles Lindberg's aerial surveys." Four years earlier, she became the first woman to earn her glider's license.

■ 1938—British travel writer, explorer, and ethnographer DAME FREYA STARK creates a list of the seven cardinal virtues that a good traveler should possess. They range from having an "unpreoccupied, observant and uncensorious mind" to "being as calmly good-tempered at the end of the day as at the beginning."

■ 1953—American aviator JACQUELINE COCHRAN becomes the first woman to fly faster than the speed of sound. She still holds more aviation records than any other pilot in history—man or woman.

■ 1957—JANE GOODALL begins a study of chimpanzees, supported by the National Geographic Society, in Africa at the Gombe Stream chimpanzee reserve.

■ 1959—In Olduvai Gorge in Tanzania, MARY LEAKEY discovers a roughly 1.8-million-year-old hominid skull. "For some reason, that skull caught the imagination," Leakey recalls in an interview, "But what it also did, and that was very important for our point of view, it caught the imagination of the National Geographic Society, and as a result they funded us for years. That was exciting."

■ 1963—Russian parachutist VALENTINA TERESHKOVA becomes the first woman in space. Twenty years later, in 1983, the first American woman SALLY RIDE, follows.

■ 1963—After participating in anthropological digs in Turkey, Iran, and Iraq, PATTY JO WATSON begins excavating Salts Cave, part of the Mammoth Cave System in Kentucky. Her groundbreaking findings revamp ideas about ancient peoples and their agricultural practices.

■ 1963—DERVLA MURPHY bicycles from Ireland to India.

■ 1970—BARBARA WASHBURN and husband, Bradford, complete a seven-year mapping project of the Grand Canyon. Barbara later receives the Centennial Medal from the National Geographic Society, for her contribution to geographic knowledge.

■ 1971—BIRUTÉ GALDIKAS departs for Borneo beginning her life studies of orangutans.

■ 1972—SYLVIA COOK and John Fairfax row across the Pacific

Ocean, a distance of 8,000 miles and a feat that takes one year.

■ 1972—Dubbed the "shark lady," underwater explorer EUGENIE CLARK publishes the first of many articles for NATIONAL GEOGRAPHIC on marine life. She writes of one expedition, "All night long [the shark] kept thumping the stern, slapping the boat amidship with its tail, and actually lifting the 32-foot craft from below…. In the end I came ashore with different feelings from those predicted by my diving friends: I believe great white sharks should be protected and that it would be a tragedy if such a magnificent animal vanished forever…."

■ 1975—JUNKO TABEI of Japan is the first woman in the world to reach the top of Mount Everest, the world's highest mountain. She is a part of a 15-woman Japanese team.

■ 1976—KRYSTYNA CHOYNOWSKI-LISKIEWICZ of Poland sails around the world by herself. The journey takes two years.

■ 1977—NAOMI JAMES sails around the world alone in nine months—the fastest time yet achieved.

■ 1978—First all-woman team ascends Annapurna under the leadership of ARLENE BLUM. They raise funds for the expedition by selling T-shirts that say "A woman's place is on top."

■ 1978—After swimming from the Bahamas to Florida, DIANA NYAD sets a world distance record. The 89-mile adventure takes 27 hours and 38 minutes to complete.

■ 1979—SYLVIA EARLE reaches a record depth of 1,250 feet (381 meters), diving in a Jim suit. She remarked, "People are under the impression that the planet is fully explored, that we've been to all the forests and climbed all the mountains. But in fact many of the forests have yet to be seen for the first time. They just happen to be under water. We're still explorers. Perhaps the greatest era is just beginning."

■ 1981—DEBRA DENKER reports in NATIONAL GEOGRAPHIC on her experiences of becoming a blood sister to a woman of the Kalash, a tribe of only 3,000 people in Pakistan. She writes, "Something very important has taken place. Whatever else I may become, I am Kalash, and an only child has found a sister."

■ 1981—The media becomes intrigued by ROBYN DAVIDSON'S journey by camel across the Gibson desert in Western Australia. The trip was in part sponsored by National Geographic. Davidson says, "I had never intended to write an account of that journey. It was a private and personal gesture which, unpredictably, became a public event—that is a depot for fantasy and distortion." Many others had died attempting similar treks into the outback.

■ 1983 — CAROL BECKWITH shares her account of life among the Wodaabe, a nomadic tribe of Niger. She details their customs of body decoration and face painting, and documents the Geerewol, a ritual of the display of male beauty.

■ 1984—Russian SVETLANA SAVITSKAYA becomes the first woman to walk in space.

■ 1984—YVA MOMATIUK and her husband JOHN EASTCOTT live among the Ngati Porou people, a major group of some 40 Maori tribes in New Zealand. They report on their stay in an article entitled "Maoris: At Home in Two Worlds" for the October 1984 issue of NATIONAL GEOGRAPHIC.

■ 1985 — DIAN FOSSEY is murdered in Rwanda's Virunga Mountains while studying mountain gorillas. Her assassins have never been caught although they are believed to have been poachers.

■ 1985 — After enduring 100 m.p.h. winds, Arctic blizzards, snow blindness, and wild animals as she raced 1,161 miles across the Alaskan wilderness, LIBBY RIDDLES becomes the first woman to win the Iditarod. "For some idiot reason the dogs trusted that I knew what I was doing."

■ 1987 — TANIA AEBI, an 18-year-old dropout, is given a challenge by her concerned father. She can either enroll in school, or he'll give her a 26-foot sloop in which she could sail around the world alone. She chose the 27,000-mile journey, braving pirates, sickness, and high seas, but ultimately finding herself along the way.

■ 1989—ARLENE BURNS fulfills a dream as she paddles the Brahmaputra River in Tibet.

■ 1990—MARGO CHISHOLM becomes the oldest woman ever to reach the summit of Mount Vinson, the highest peak on the continent of Antarctica, and the third summit on her quest to reach the top of the highest mountain on each of the seven continents.

■ 1990—SUSAN BUTCHER wins the Iditarod for the fourth time. She sets a new course record—11 days, 1 hour, and 53 minutes.

■ 1991—French volcanologist KATIA KRAFFT is killed by an eruption of Japan's Unzen volcano along with her husband Maurice, after 20 years studying and photographing erupting volcanoes all over the world together. Katia remarked, "the volcanoes are our children…sometimes very nasty, spoiled children that demand all our attention."

■ 1992—MAE JEMISON spends eight days in space as part one of the crew of the space shuttle *Endeavour*. She not only is the first African-American astronaut, but also has worked in Cambodia with refugees, and served as a Peace Corps medic in Africa.

■ 1993 — LYNN HILL "frees the nose"— becoming the first person to free-climb the nose route of El Capitan, in Yosemite Valley, California.

■ 1993 — Anthropologist CYNTHIA BEALL and husband, Melvyn Goldstein, document the life of Mongolian nomads.

■ 1995—HELEN THAYER and her husband, Bill, trek and kayak 1,200 miles into remote areas of Brazilian rain forest. When their trip ends, they comment, "It was difficult for us to re-enter the bustling, busy, noisy world of the city…. We thought back to the Indians we had befriended. We envied them their lifestyle of peace and quiet in the jungle."

■ 1996 — SHANNON LUCID returns to Earth after spending six months serving on Russia's space station *Mir*. Lucid holds an international record for the most hours in orbit by any woman in the world.

■ 1997 — After three years of planning, CATHERINE DESTIVELLE is the first to climb a 2,600-foot ice fall in Nepal.

■ 1999—EILEEN COLLINS, veteran of more than 537 hours in space, serves as the first female shuttle commander aboard the STS-93 *Columbia*. The mission deployed the Chandra X-Ray Observatory, designed to conduct comprehensive studies of the universe.

■ 1999—Adventurer and photographer NEVADA WIER hikes and rafts the length of the Blue Nile in Ethiopia. She explains, "It was not enough to travel the length of the Blue Nile, it was more important to delve into the cultures along the journey… I feel that I am as much of an ambassador as I am an explorer…."

■ 2000—Ninety-year-old DORIS HADDOCK of New Hampshire walks 3,200 miles from Los Angeles to the Capitol Steps in Washington, D.C. to raise support for campaign finance reform.

■ 2000—LIV ARNESEN and ANN BANCROFT begin their expedition to cross Antarctica in November. Ann Bancroft states, "We believe this journey stands for hope—hope that other seemingly impossible goals can be met by people everywhere."

ACKNOWLEDGMENTS

The Book Division wishes to thank the following people and organizations for their photographs, which assisted in creating the art for this book: National Archives, Helen Thayer, Hulton Getty, Guy Martin-Ravel, Barry Tessman, John Eastcott/Yva Momatiuk, Bob Campbell, Rod Brindamour, Brian Pearce, NASA, Library of Congress, Natalie Fobes. We also wish to acknowledge Rebecca Martin who helped make this book possible.

PUBLISHED BY
THE NATIONAL GEOGRAPHIC SOCIETY

John M. Fahey, Jr., *President and Chief Executive Officer*
Gilbert M.Grosvenor, *Chairman of the Board*
Nina D.Hoffman, *Senior Vice President*
William R. Gray, *Vice President and Director, Book Division*
Charles Kogod, *Assistant Director*
Barbara A. Payne, *Editorial Director and Managing Editor*

STAFF FOR THIS BOOK
Dale-Marie Herring, *Project Editor*
Suez Kehl, *Art Director*
Johnna M. Rizzo, *Researcher*
Carl Mehler, *Director of Maps*
R. Gary Colbert, *Production Director*
Richard S. Wain, *Production Project Manager*
Deborah E. Patton, *Indexer*
George V. White,
Manufacturing and Quality Control, Director

INDEX

Boldface indicates illustrations.

MICHELE SLUNG is a woman of many parts. A journalist, humorist, anthologist, editor, former bookseller, and frequent reviewer, she is author herself of more than a dozen books, among them several best-sellers that have appeared in translation around the world. She currently contributes the feature "Read with Tea," on the lore and love of books, to *Victoria* magazine. She has written for the *New York Times*, the *Washington Post*, the *New Republic*, *USA Today*, *Ms.*, and *Conde Nast Traveler*, among other publications.